MARVEL

AVENGERS
ULTRON REVOLUTION

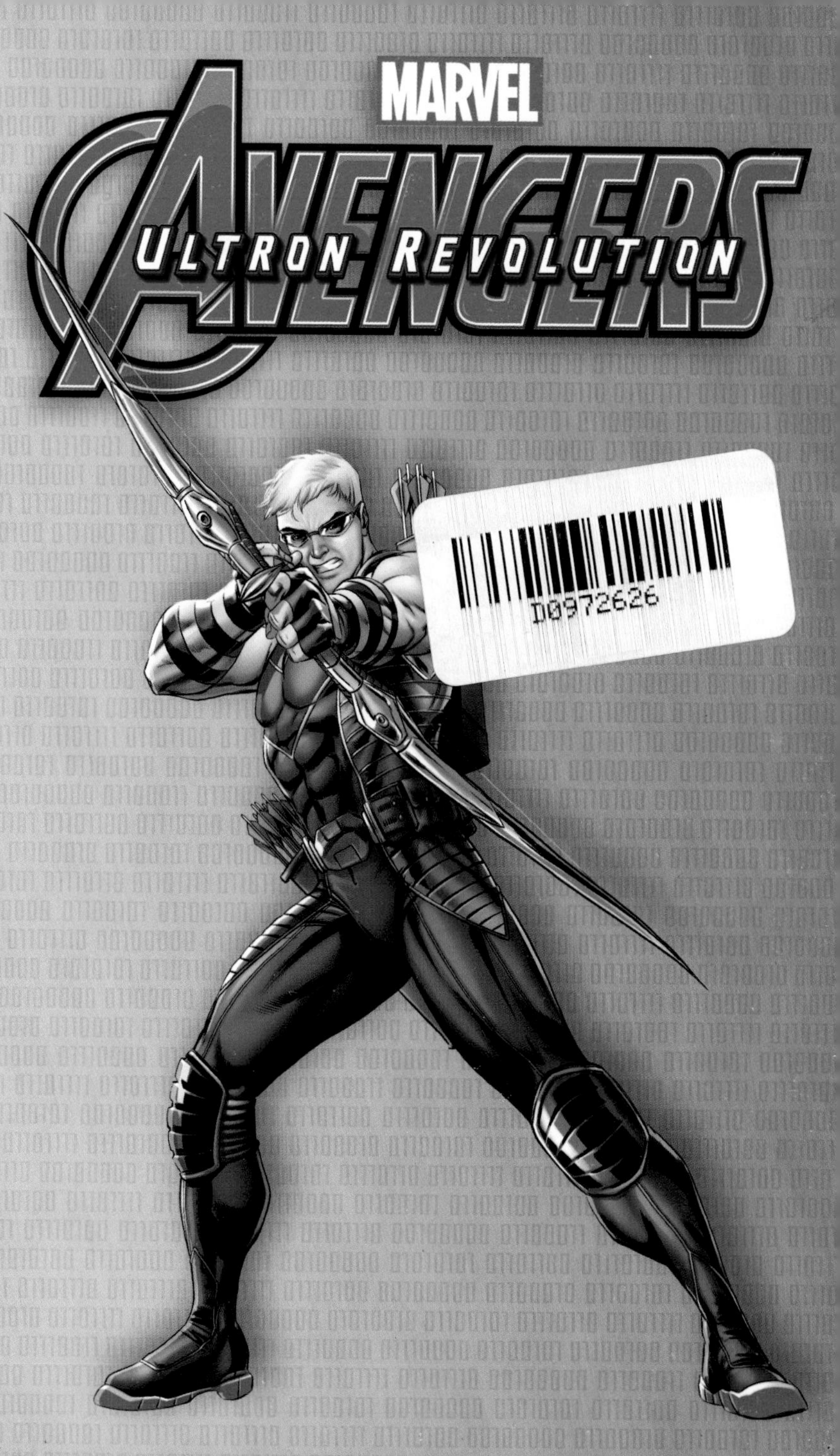

MARVEL UNIVERSE AVENGERS: ULTRON REVOLUTION VOL. 2. Contains material originally published in magazine form as MARVEL UNIVERSE AVENGERS: ULTRON REVOLUTION #5-8. First printing 2017. ISBN# 978-1-302-90256-8. Published by MARVEL WORLDWIDE, INC., a subsidiary of MARVEL ENTERTAINMENT, LLC. OFFICE OF PUBLICATION: 135 West 50th Street, New York, NY 10020. Copyright © 2017 MARVEL. No similarity between any of the names, characters, persons, and/or institutions in this magazine with those of any living or dead person or institution is intended, and any such similarity which may exist is purely coincidental. **Printed in the U.S.A.** ALAN FINE, President, Marvel Entertainment; DAN BUCKLEY, President, TV, Publishing & Brand Management; JOE QUESADA, Chief Creative Officer; TOM BREVOORT, SVP of Publishing; DAVID BOGART, SVP of Business Affairs & Operations, Publishing & Partnership; C.B. CEBULSKI, VP of Brand Management & Development, Asia; DAVID GABRIEL, SVP of Sales & Marketing, Publishing; JEFF YOUNGQUIST, VP of Production & Special Projects; DAN CARR, Executive Director of Publishing Technology; ALEX MORALES, Director of Publishing Operations; SUSAN CRESPI, Production Manager; STAN LEE, Chairman Emeritus. For information regarding advertising in Marvel Comics or on Marvel.com, please contact Vit DeBellis, Integrated Sales Manager, at vdebellis@marvel.com. For Marvel subscription inquiries, please call 888-511-5480. **Manufactured between 1/20/2017 and 2/21/2017 by SHERIDAN, CHELSEA, MI, USA.**

10 9 8 7 6 5 4 3 2 1

MARVEL
AVENGERS
ULTRON REVOLUTION

Based on the TV series written by
**MATT WAYNE, MARK HOFFMEIER,
KEVIN SHINICK & MARK BANKER**

Directed by
**TIM ELDRED &
PHIL PIGNOTTI**

Art by
**MARVEL ANIMATION
STUDIOS**

Adapted by
JOE CARAMAGNA

Special Thanks to
**HANNAH MacDONALD &
PRODUCT FACTORY**

Editor
CHRISTINA HARRINGTON

Senior Editor
MARK PANICCIA

Avengers created by **STAN LEE & JACK KIRBY**

Collection Editor: JENNIFER GRÜNWALD
Associate Managing Editor: KATERI WOODY
Assistant Editor: CAITLIN O'CONNELL
Editor, Special Projects: MARK D. BEAZLEY

VP Production & Special Projects: JEFF YOUNGQUIST
SVP Print, Sales & Marketing: DAVID GABRIEL
Head of Marvel Television: JEPH LOEB
Book Designer: ADAM DEL RE

Editor in Chief: AXEL ALONSO
Chief Creative Officer: JOE QUESADA
Publisher: DAN BUCKLEY
Executive Producer: ALAN FINE

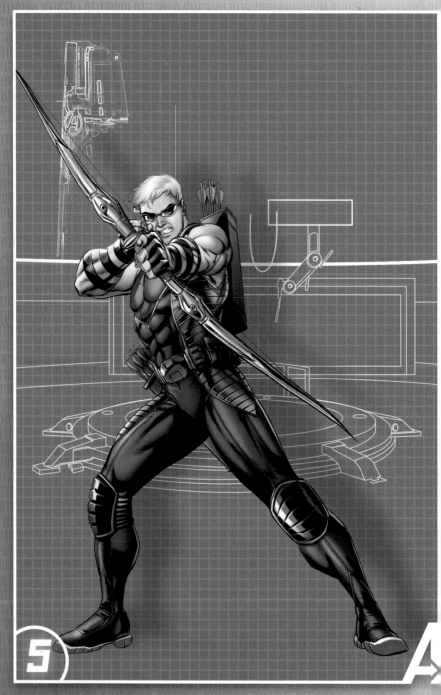

5

UNDER SIEGE

The AVENGERS have sworn to protect the world against the nefarious plots of the Red Skull, Thanos, Ultron, and Baron Zemo. Made up from real-life geniuses, super spies, an ancient god and one ridiculously strong green dude, you might wonder how a simple archer like CLINT BARTON, AKA HAWKEYE, could possibly fit on the roster.

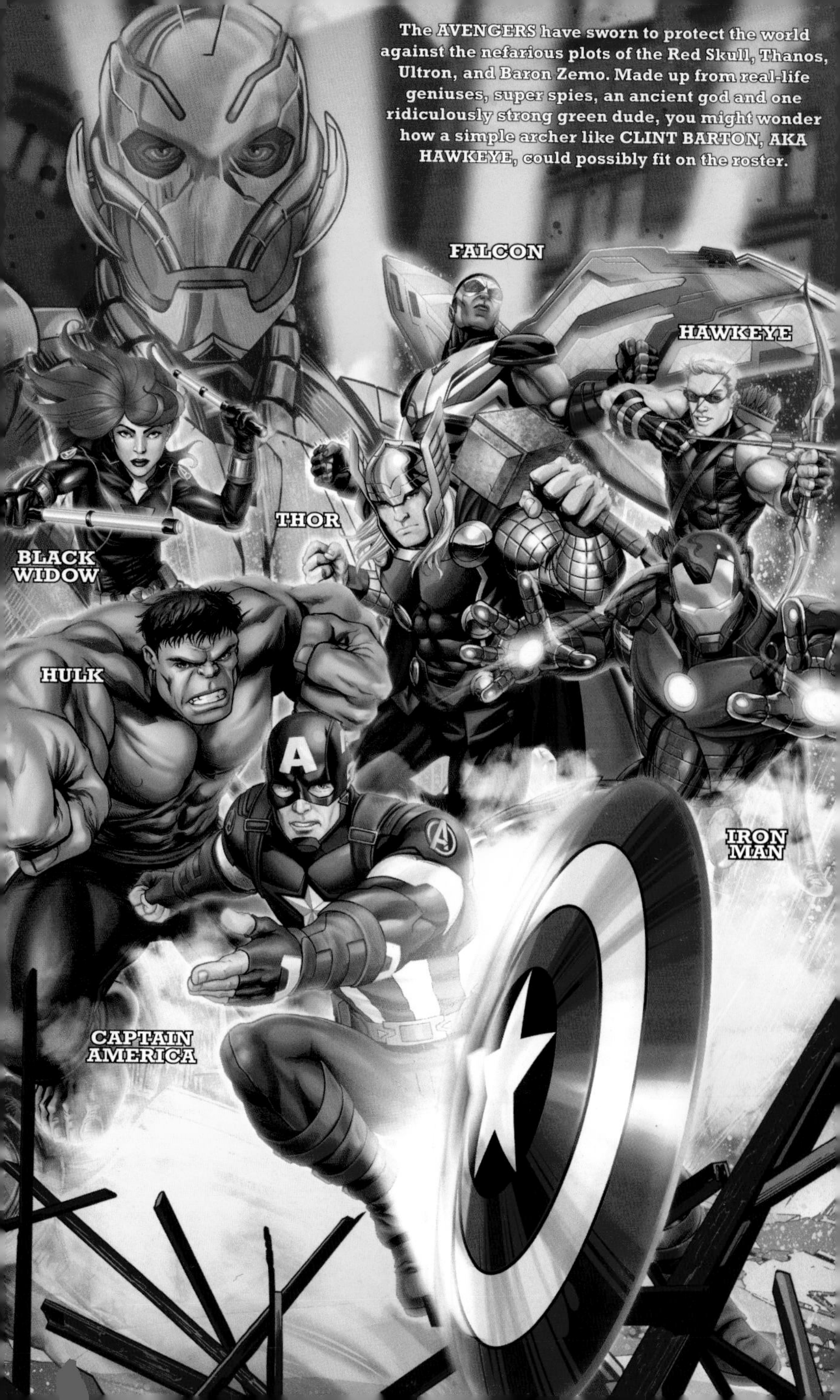
FALCON
HAWKEYE
BLACK WIDOW
THOR
HULK
IRON MAN
CAPTAIN AMERICA

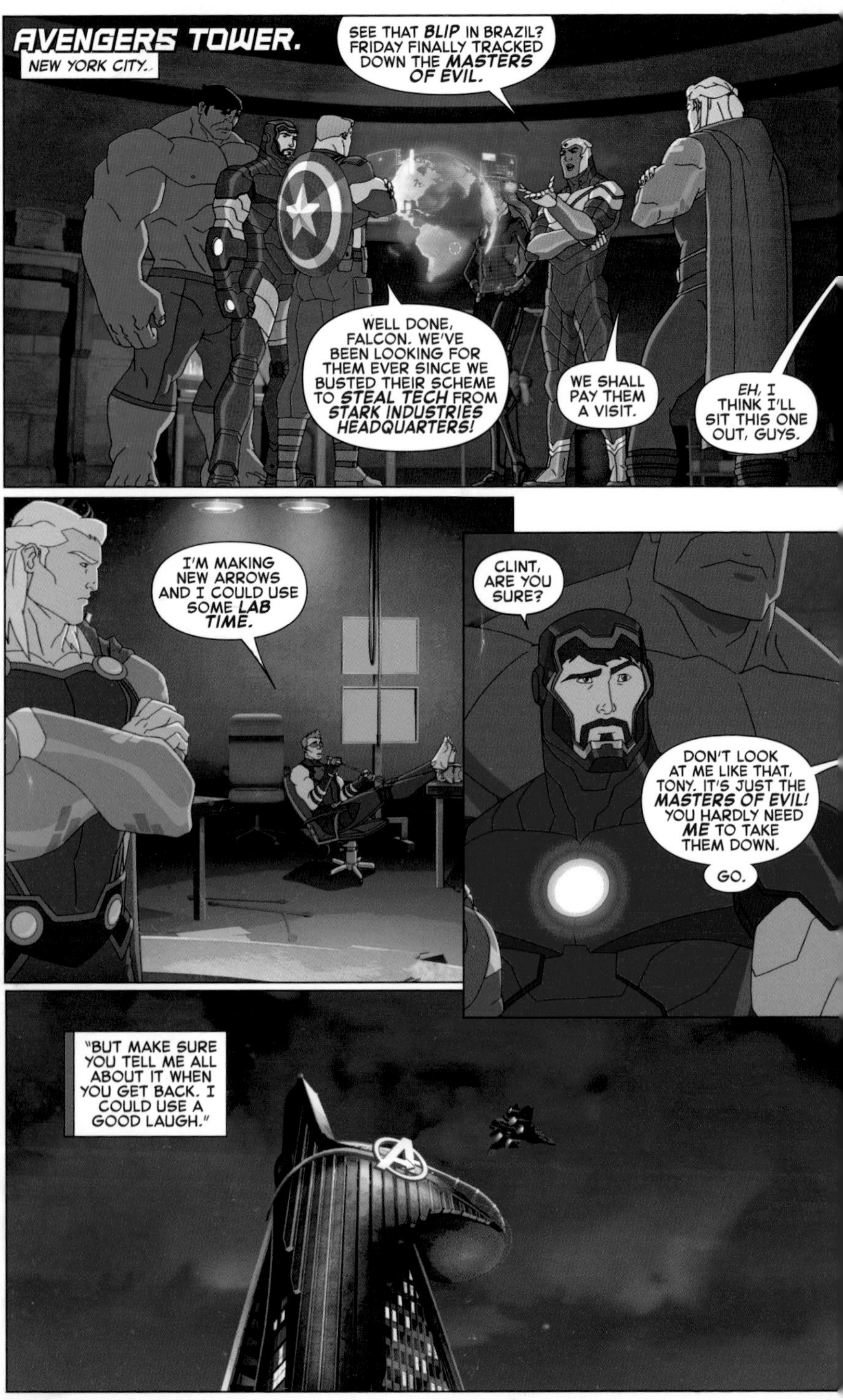
AVENGERS TOWER.
NEW YORK CITY.
SEE THAT BLIP IN BRAZIL? FRIDAY FINALLY TRACKED DOWN THE MASTERS OF EVIL.
WELL DONE, FALCON. WE'VE BEEN LOOKING FOR THEM EVER SINCE WE BUSTED THEIR SCHEME TO STEAL TECH FROM STARK INDUSTRIES HEADQUARTERS!
WE SHALL PAY THEM A VISIT.
EH, I THINK I'LL SIT THIS ONE OUT, GUYS.
I'M MAKING NEW ARROWS AND I COULD USE SOME LAB TIME.
CLINT, ARE YOU SURE?
DON'T LOOK AT ME LIKE THAT, TONY. IT'S JUST THE MASTERS OF EVIL! YOU HARDLY NEED ME TO TAKE THEM DOWN.
GO.
"BUT MAKE SURE YOU TELL ME ALL ABOUT IT WHEN YOU GET BACK. I COULD USE A GOOD LAUGH."

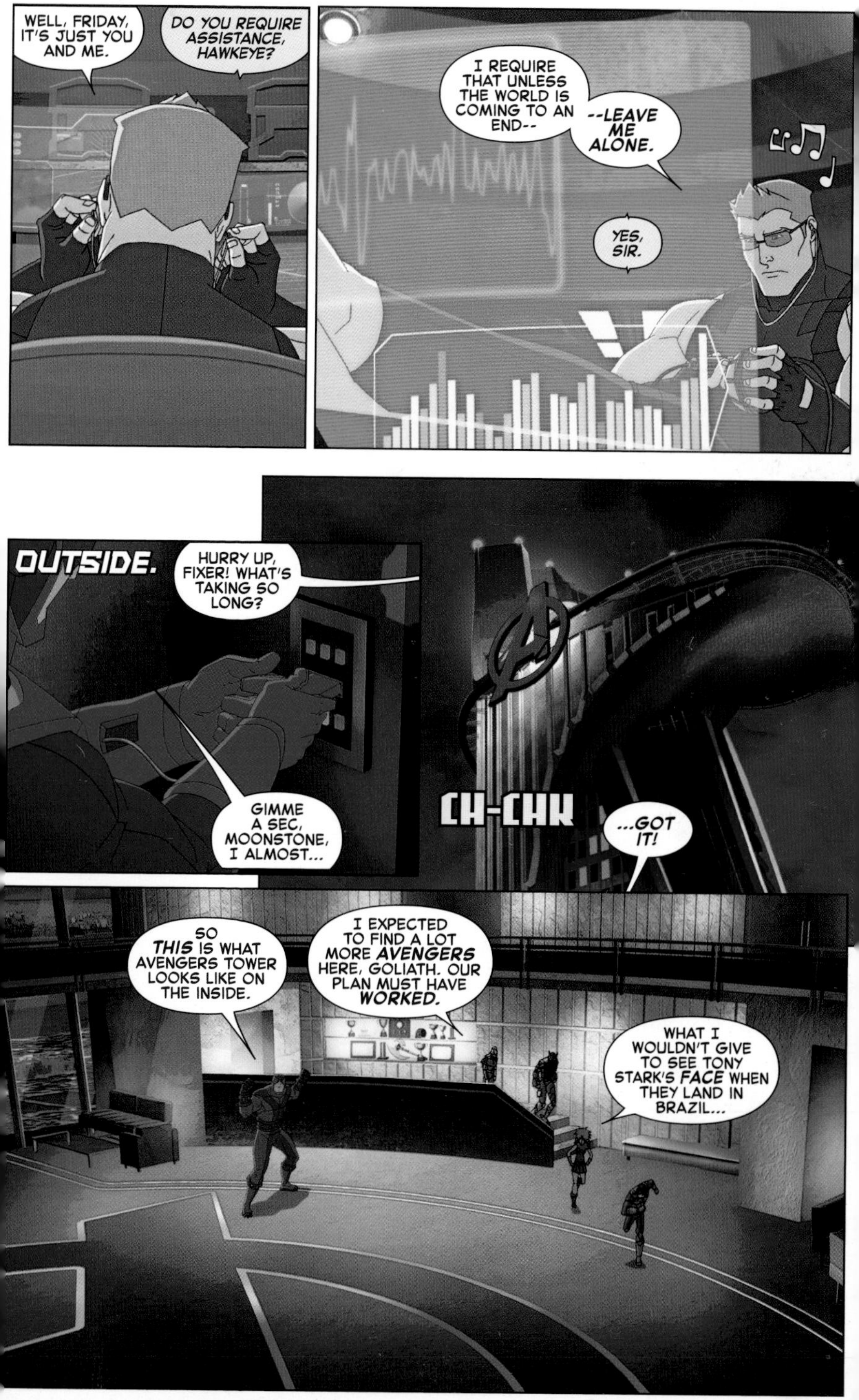

WELL, FRIDAY, IT'S JUST YOU AND ME.
DO YOU REQUIRE ASSISTANCE, HAWKEYE?
I REQUIRE THAT UNLESS THE WORLD IS COMING TO AN END--
--LEAVE ME ALONE.
YES, SIR.
OUTSIDE.
HURRY UP, FIXER! WHAT'S TAKING SO LONG?
GIMME A SEC, MOONSTONE, I ALMOST...
CH-CHK
...GOT IT!
SO THIS IS WHAT AVENGERS TOWER LOOKS LIKE ON THE INSIDE.
I EXPECTED TO FIND A LOT MORE AVENGERS HERE, GOLIATH. OUR PLAN MUST HAVE WORKED.
WHAT I WOULDN'T GIVE TO SEE TONY STARK'S FACE WHEN THEY LAND IN BRAZIL...

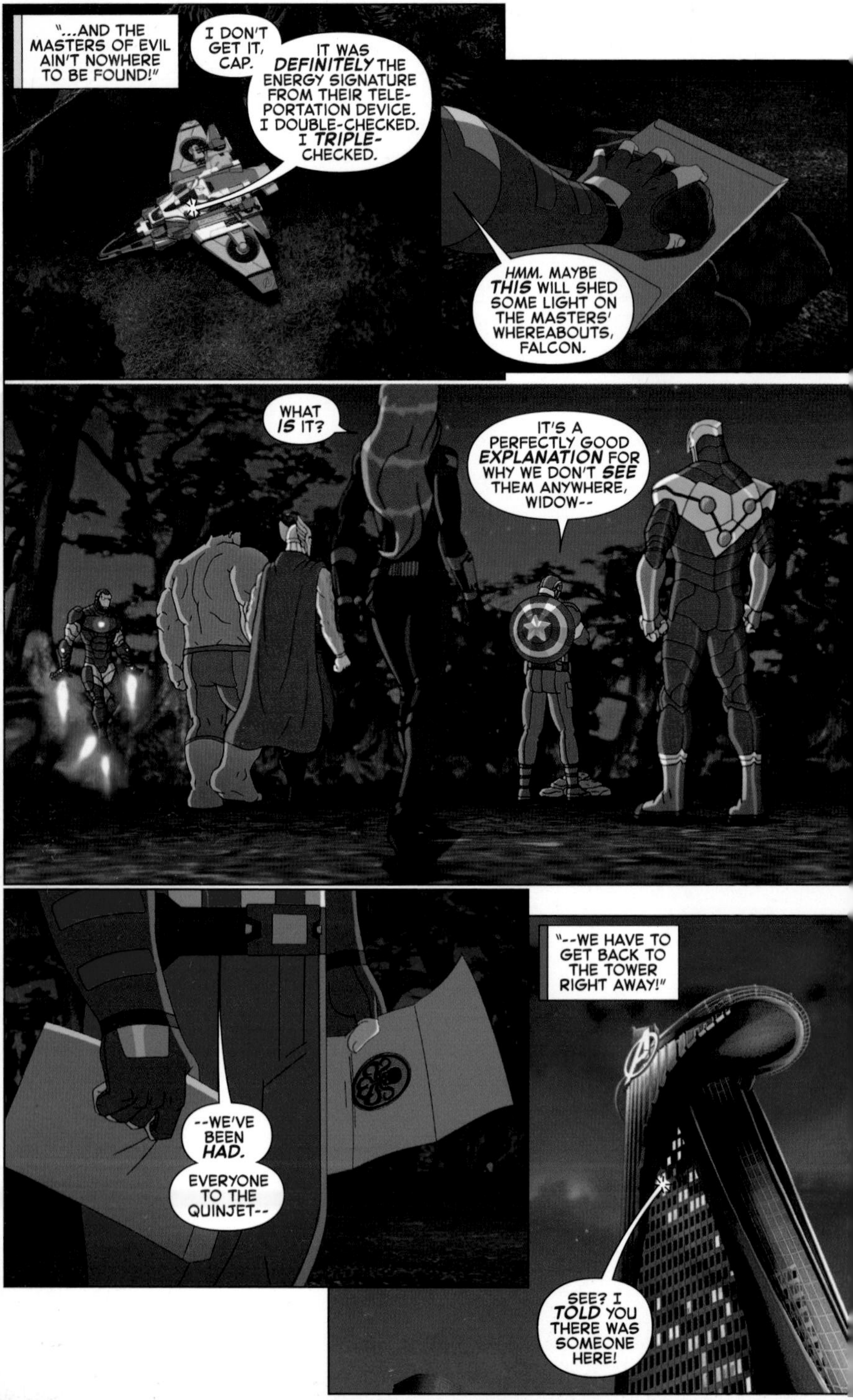
"...AND THE MASTERS OF EVIL AIN'T NOWHERE TO BE FOUND!"
I DON'T GET IT, CAP.
IT WAS DEFINITELY THE ENERGY SIGNATURE FROM THEIR TELE-PORTATION DEVICE. I DOUBLE-CHECKED. I TRIPLE-CHECKED.
HMM. MAYBE THIS WILL SHED SOME LIGHT ON THE MASTERS' WHEREABOUTS, FALCON.
WHAT IS IT?
IT'S A PERFECTLY GOOD EXPLANATION FOR WHY WE DON'T SEE THEM ANYWHERE, WIDOW--
--WE'VE BEEN HAD.
EVERYONE TO THE QUINJET--
"--WE HAVE TO GET BACK TO THE TOWER RIGHT AWAY!"
SEE? I TOLD YOU THERE WAS SOMEONE HERE!

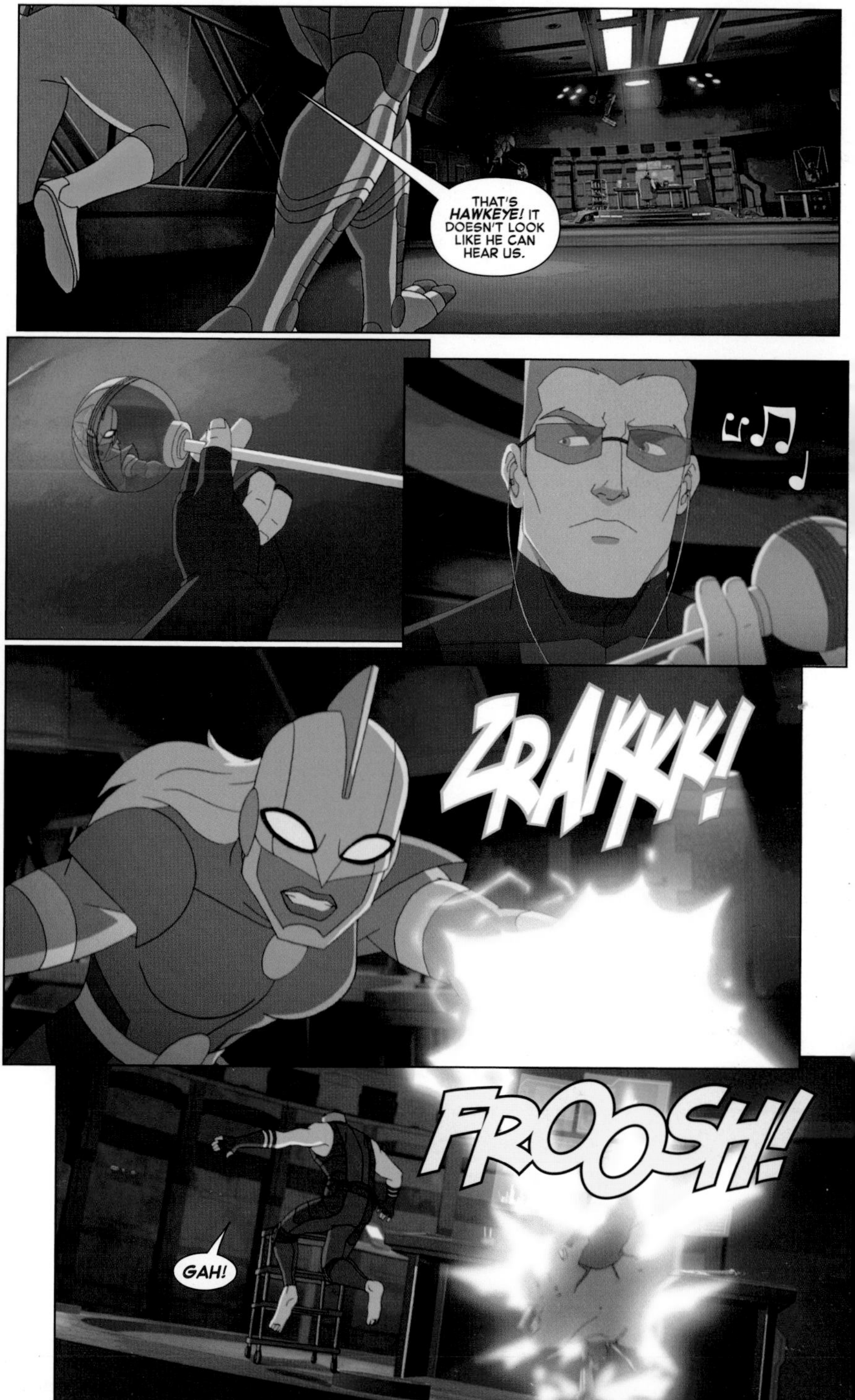
THAT'S *HAWKEYE!* IT DOESN'T LOOK LIKE HE CAN HEAR US.
ZRAKKK!
FROOSH!
GAH!

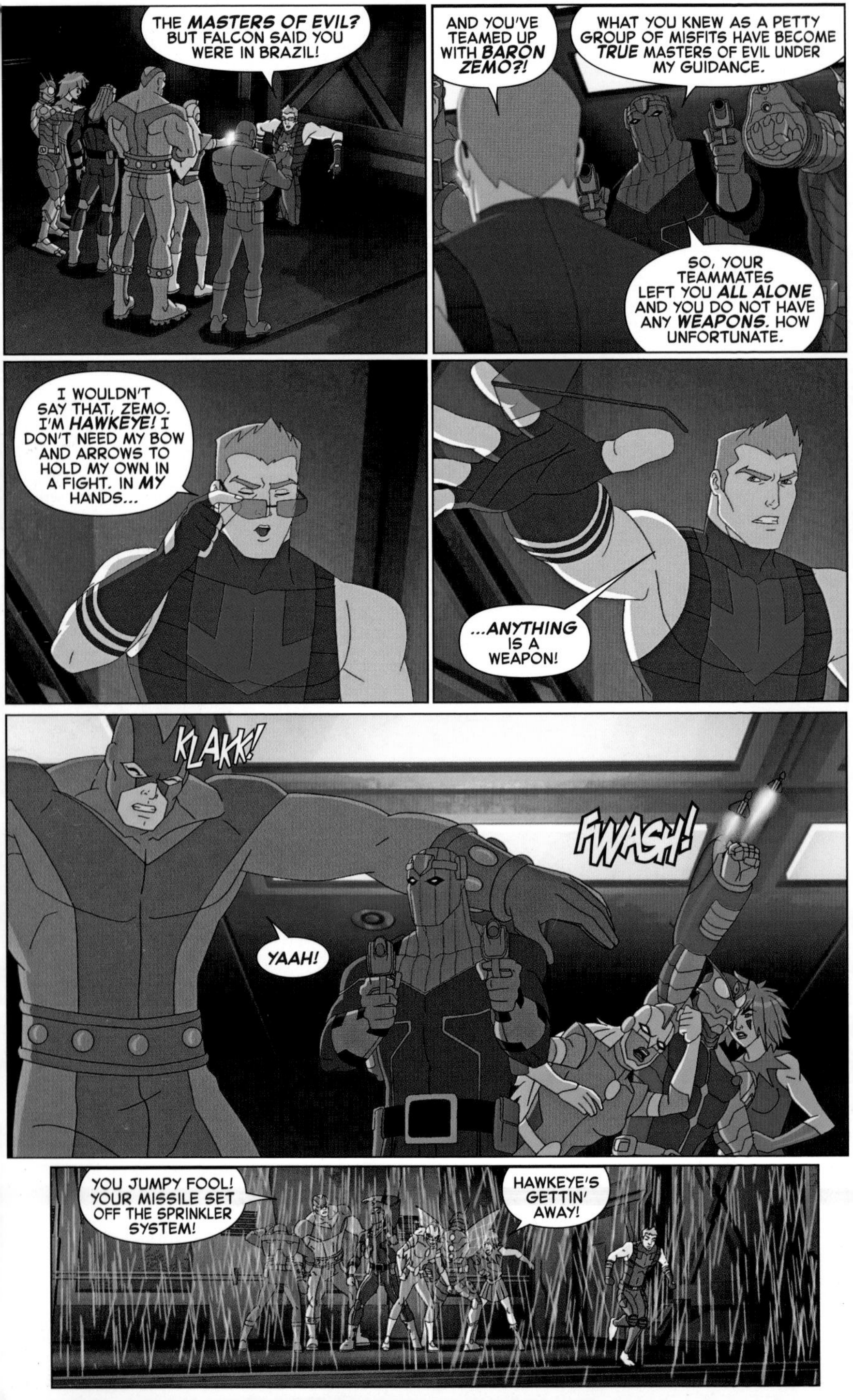
THE MASTERS OF EVIL? BUT FALCON SAID YOU WERE IN BRAZIL!
AND YOU'VE TEAMED UP WITH BARON ZEMO?!
WHAT YOU KNEW AS A PETTY GROUP OF MISFITS HAVE BECOME TRUE MASTERS OF EVIL UNDER MY GUIDANCE.
SO, YOUR TEAMMATES LEFT YOU ALL ALONE AND YOU DO NOT HAVE ANY WEAPONS. HOW UNFORTUNATE.
I WOULDN'T SAY THAT, ZEMO. I'M HAWKEYE! I DON'T NEED MY BOW AND ARROWS TO HOLD MY OWN IN A FIGHT. IN MY HANDS...
...ANYTHING IS A WEAPON!
KLAKK!
FWASH!
YAAH!
YOU JUMPY FOOL! YOUR MISSILE SET OFF THE SPRINKLER SYSTEM!
HAWKEYE'S GETTIN' AWAY!

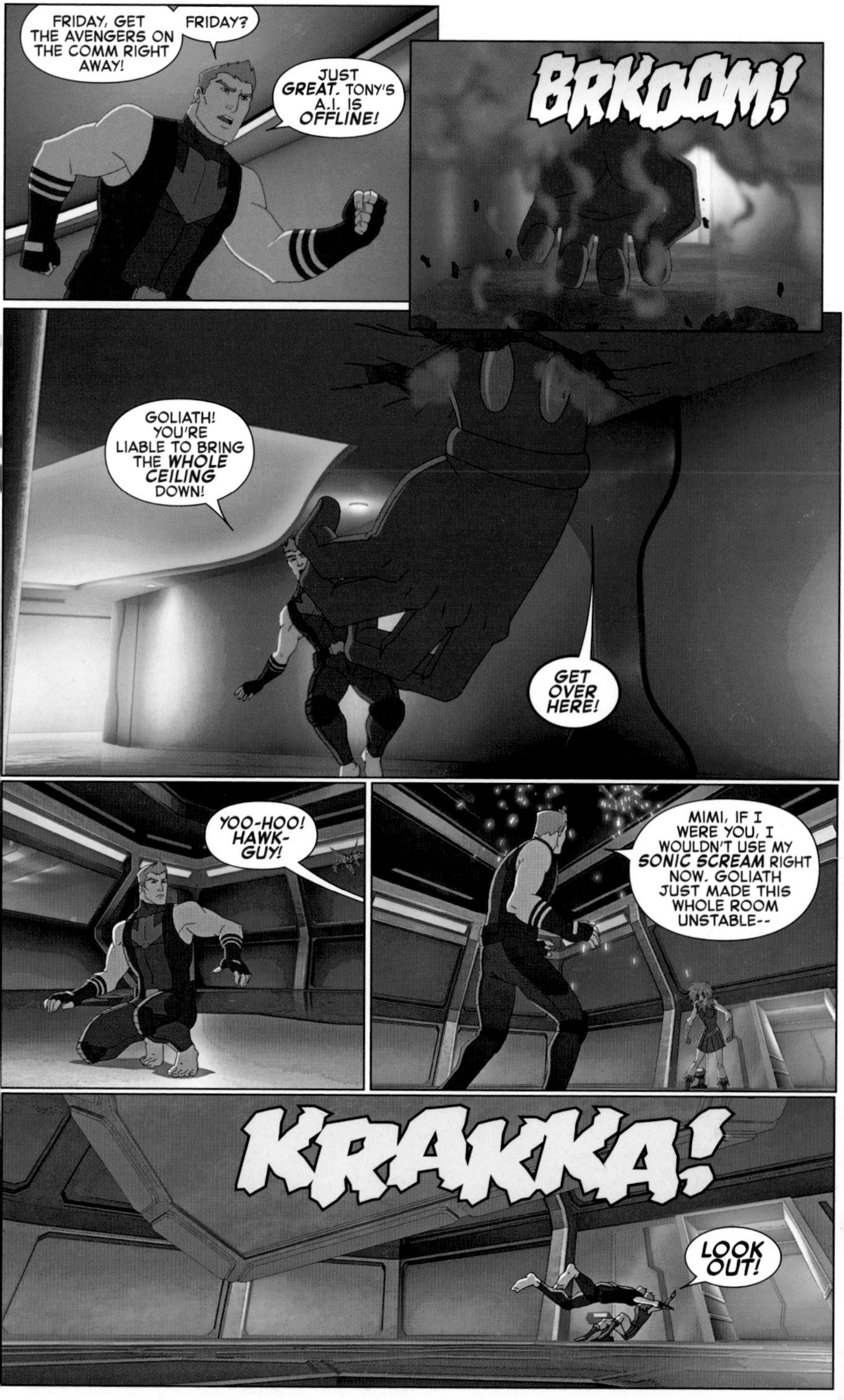

FRIDAY, GET THE AVENGERS ON THE COMM RIGHT AWAY!
FRIDAY?
JUST GREAT. TONY'S A.I. IS OFFLINE!
BRKOOM!
GOLIATH! YOU'RE LIABLE TO BRING THE WHOLE CEILING DOWN!
GET OVER HERE!
YOO-HOO! HAWK-GUY!
MIMI, IF I WERE YOU, I WOULDN'T USE MY SONIC SCREAM RIGHT NOW. GOLIATH JUST MADE THIS WHOLE ROOM UNSTABLE--
KRAKKA!
LOOK OUT!

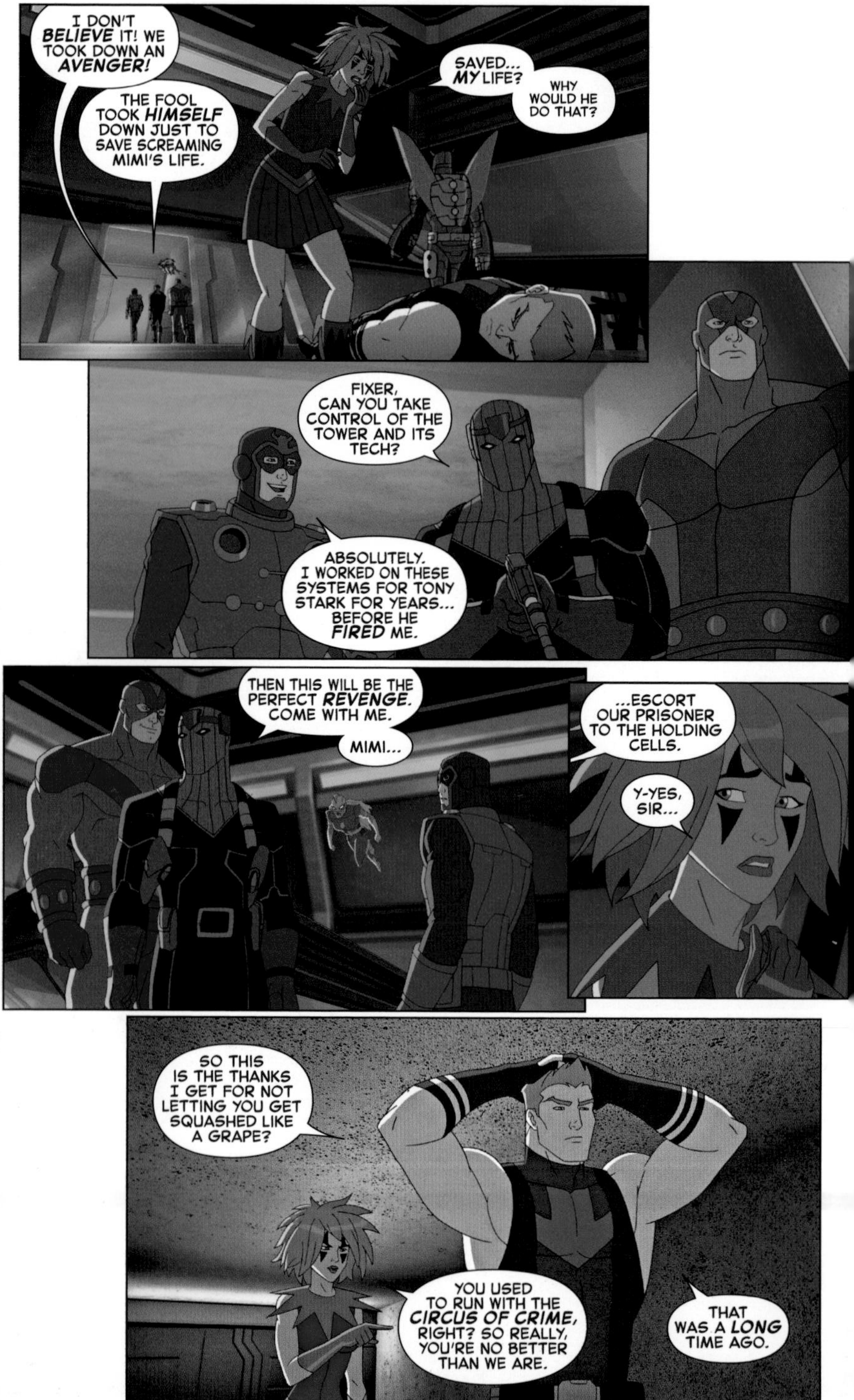

I DON'T BELIEVE IT! WE TOOK DOWN AN AVENGER!
THE FOOL TOOK HIMSELF DOWN JUST TO SAVE SCREAMING MIMI'S LIFE.
SAVED... MY LIFE?
WHY WOULD HE DO THAT?
FIXER, CAN YOU TAKE CONTROL OF THE TOWER AND ITS TECH?
ABSOLUTELY. I WORKED ON THESE SYSTEMS FOR TONY STARK FOR YEARS... BEFORE HE FIRED ME.
THEN THIS WILL BE THE PERFECT REVENGE. COME WITH ME.
MIMI...
...ESCORT OUR PRISONER TO THE HOLDING CELLS.
Y-YES, SIR...
SO THIS IS THE THANKS I GET FOR NOT LETTING YOU GET SQUASHED LIKE A GRAPE?
YOU USED TO RUN WITH THE CIRCUS OF CRIME, RIGHT? SO REALLY, YOU'RE NO BETTER THAN WE ARE.
THAT WAS A LONG TIME AGO.

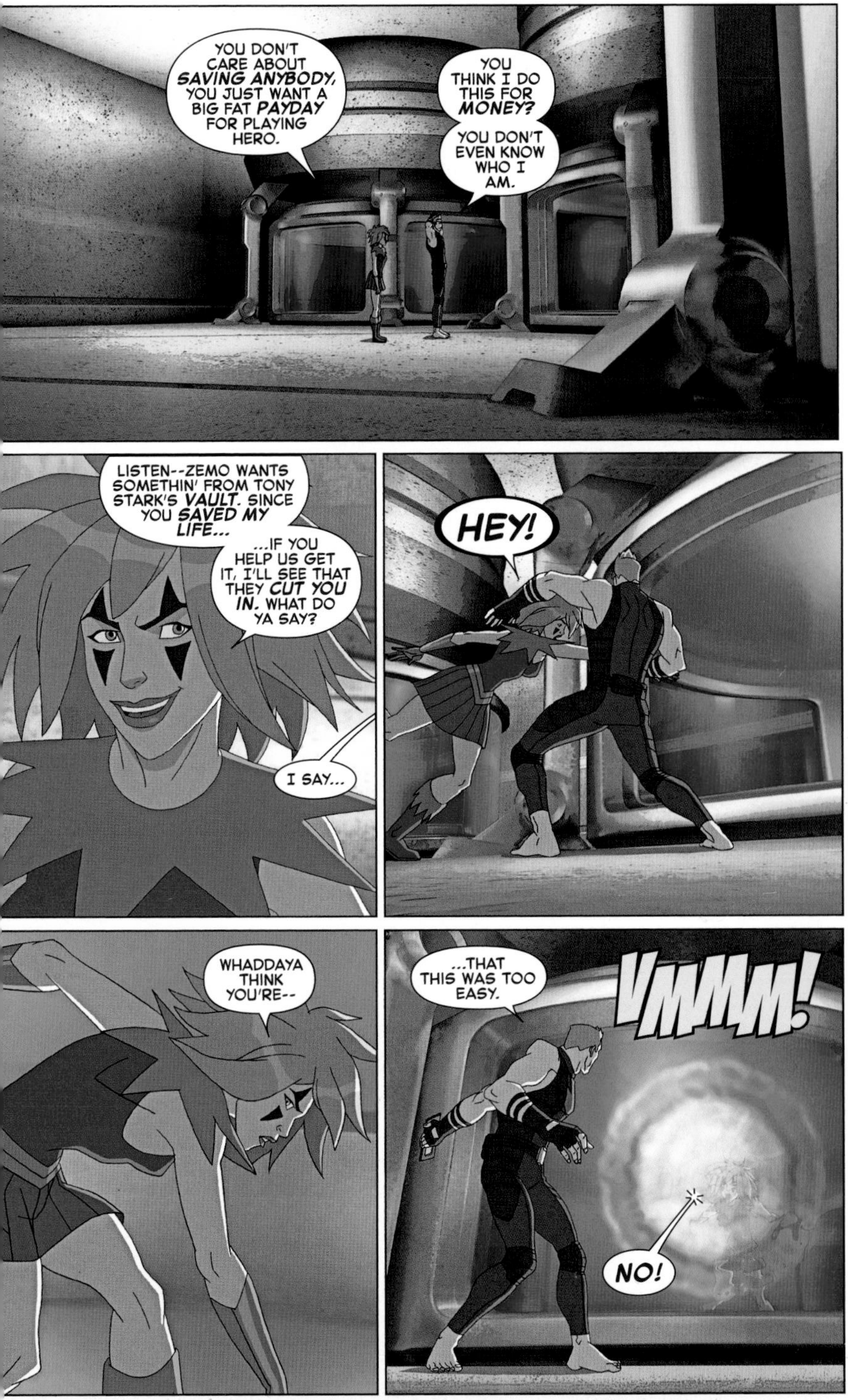

YOU DON'T CARE ABOUT SAVING ANYBODY. YOU JUST WANT A BIG FAT PAYDAY FOR PLAYING HERO.
YOU THINK I DO THIS FOR MONEY?
YOU DON'T EVEN KNOW WHO I AM.
LISTEN--ZEMO WANTS SOMETHIN' FROM TONY STARK'S VAULT. SINCE YOU SAVED MY LIFE...
...IF YOU HELP US GET IT, I'LL SEE THAT THEY CUT YOU IN. WHAT DO YA SAY?
I SAY...
HEY!
WHADDAYA THINK YOU'RE--
...THAT THIS WAS TOO EASY.
VMMMM!
NO!

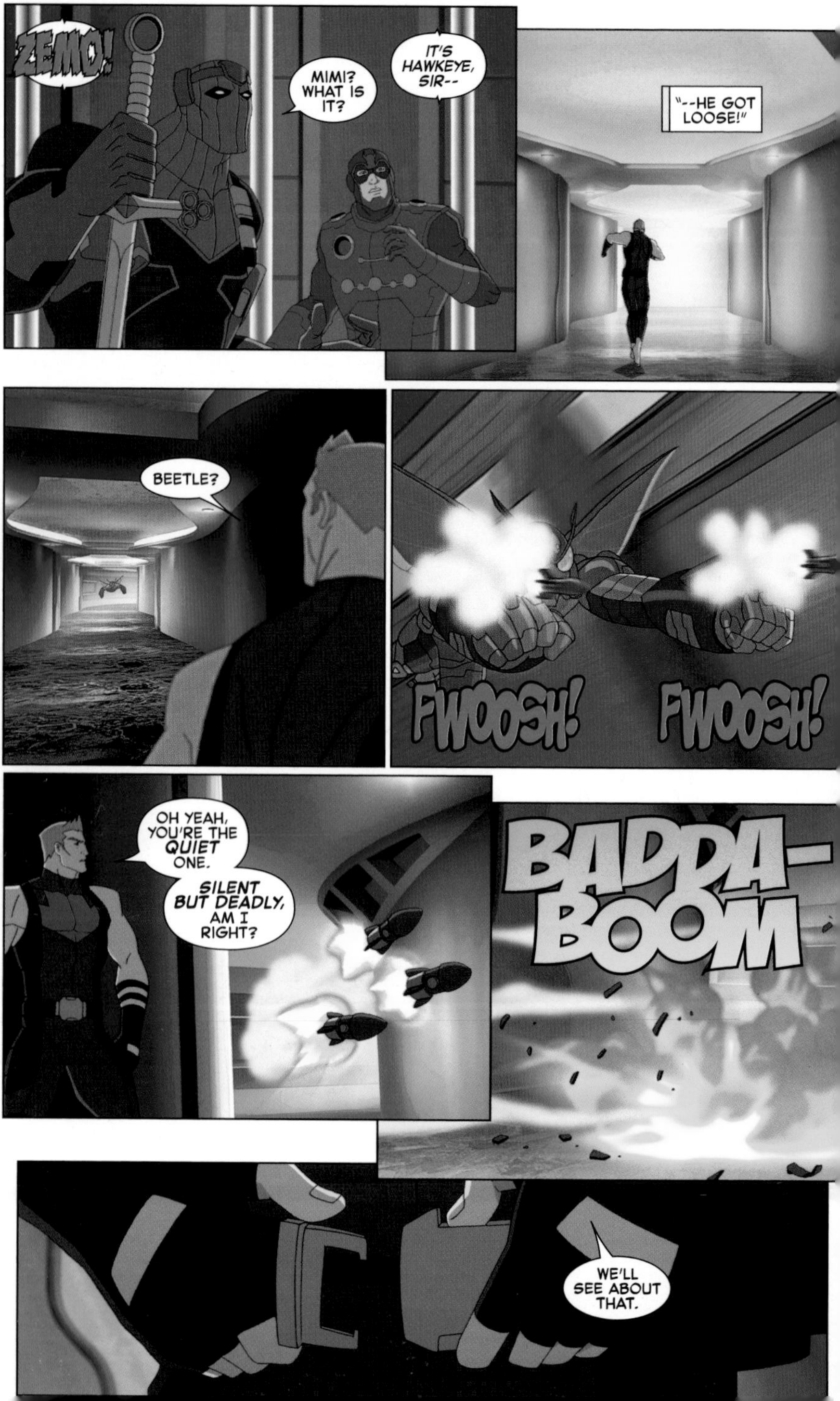
ZEMO!
MIMI? WHAT IS IT?
IT'S HAWKEYE, SIR--
"--HE GOT LOOSE!"
BEETLE?
FWOOSH!
FWOOSH!
OH YEAH, YOU'RE THE QUIET ONE.
SILENT BUT DEADLY, AM I RIGHT?
BADDA-BOOM
WE'LL SEE ABOUT THAT.

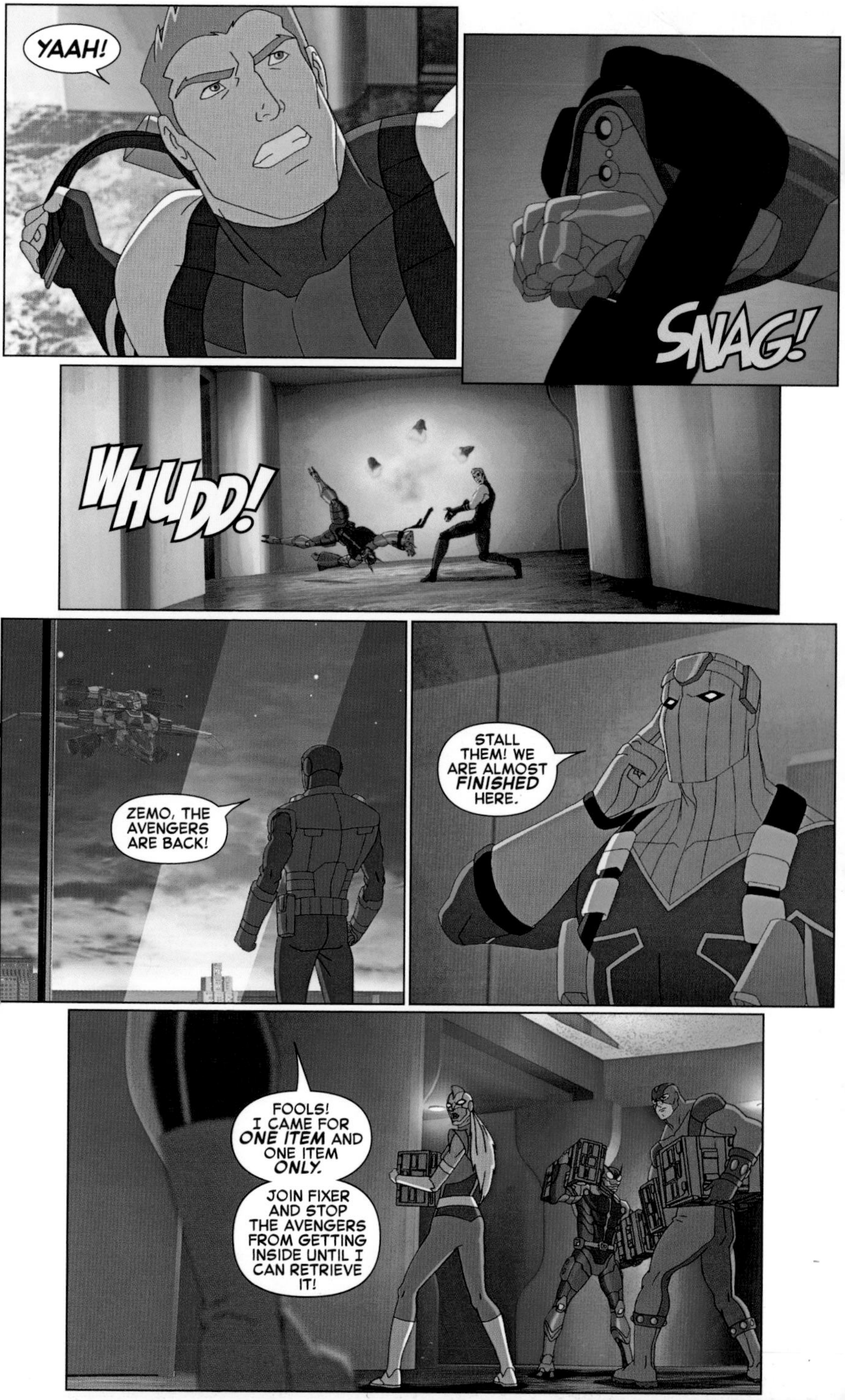
YAAH!
SNAG!
WHUDD!
ZEMO, THE AVENGERS ARE BACK!
STALL THEM! WE ARE ALMOST FINISHED HERE.
FOOLS! I CAME FOR ONE ITEM AND ONE ITEM ONLY.
JOIN FIXER AND STOP THE AVENGERS FROM GETTING INSIDE UNTIL I CAN RETRIEVE IT!

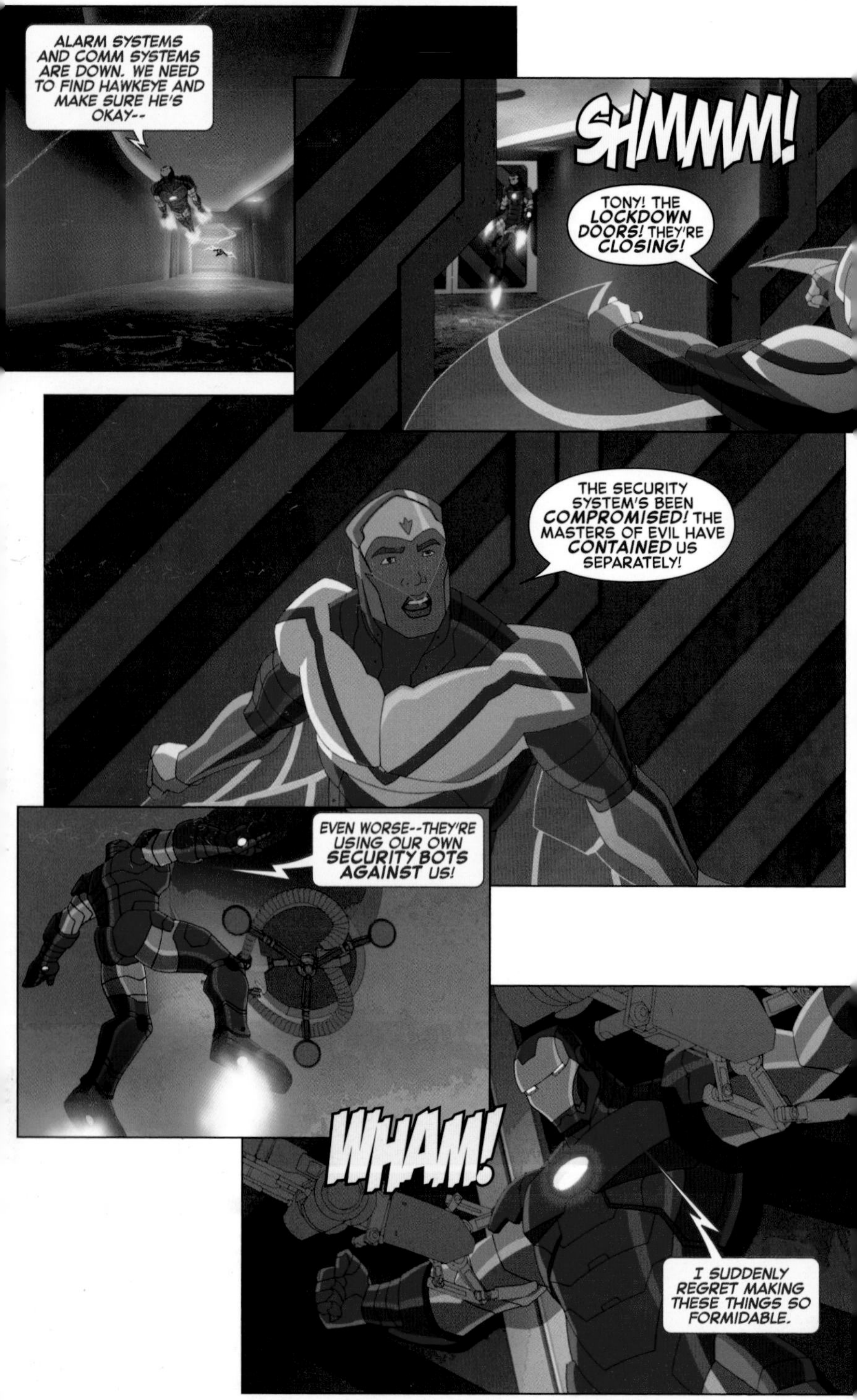

ALARM SYSTEMS AND COMM SYSTEMS ARE DOWN. WE NEED TO FIND HAWKEYE AND MAKE SURE HE'S OKAY--
SHMMM!
TONY! THE LOCKDOWN DOORS! THEY'RE CLOSING!
THE SECURITY SYSTEM'S BEEN COMPROMISED! THE MASTERS OF EVIL HAVE CONTAINED US SEPARATELY!
EVEN WORSE--THEY'RE USING OUR OWN SECURITY BOTS AGAINST US!
WHAM!
I SUDDENLY REGRET MAKING THESE THINGS SO FORMIDABLE.

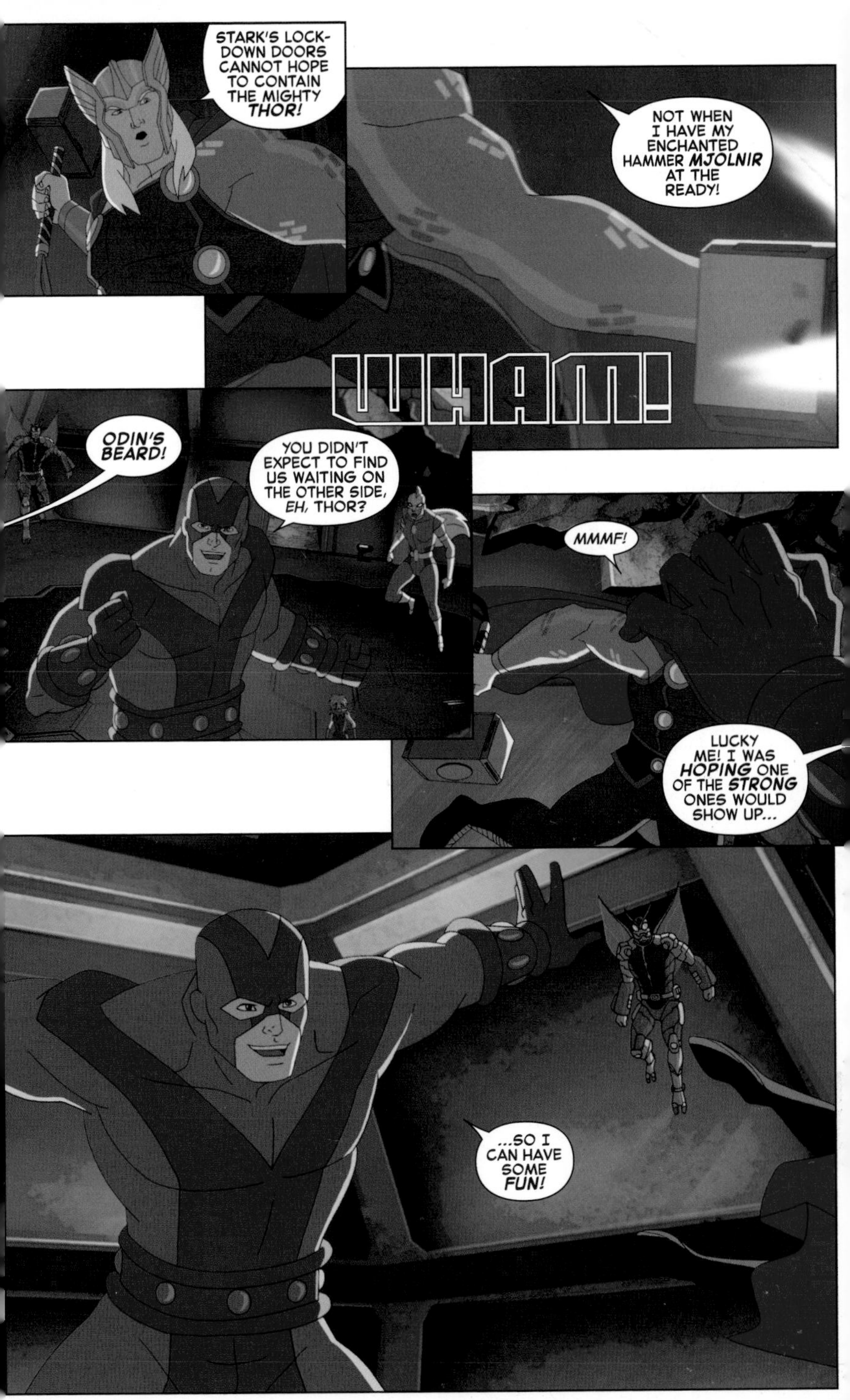

STARK'S LOCK-DOWN DOORS CANNOT HOPE TO CONTAIN THE MIGHTY THOR!
NOT WHEN I HAVE MY ENCHANTED HAMMER MJOLNIR AT THE READY!
WHAM!
ODIN'S BEARD!
YOU DIDN'T EXPECT TO FIND US WAITING ON THE OTHER SIDE, EH, THOR?
MMMF!
LUCKY ME! I WAS HOPING ONE OF THE STRONG ONES WOULD SHOW UP...
...SO I CAN HAVE SOME FUN!

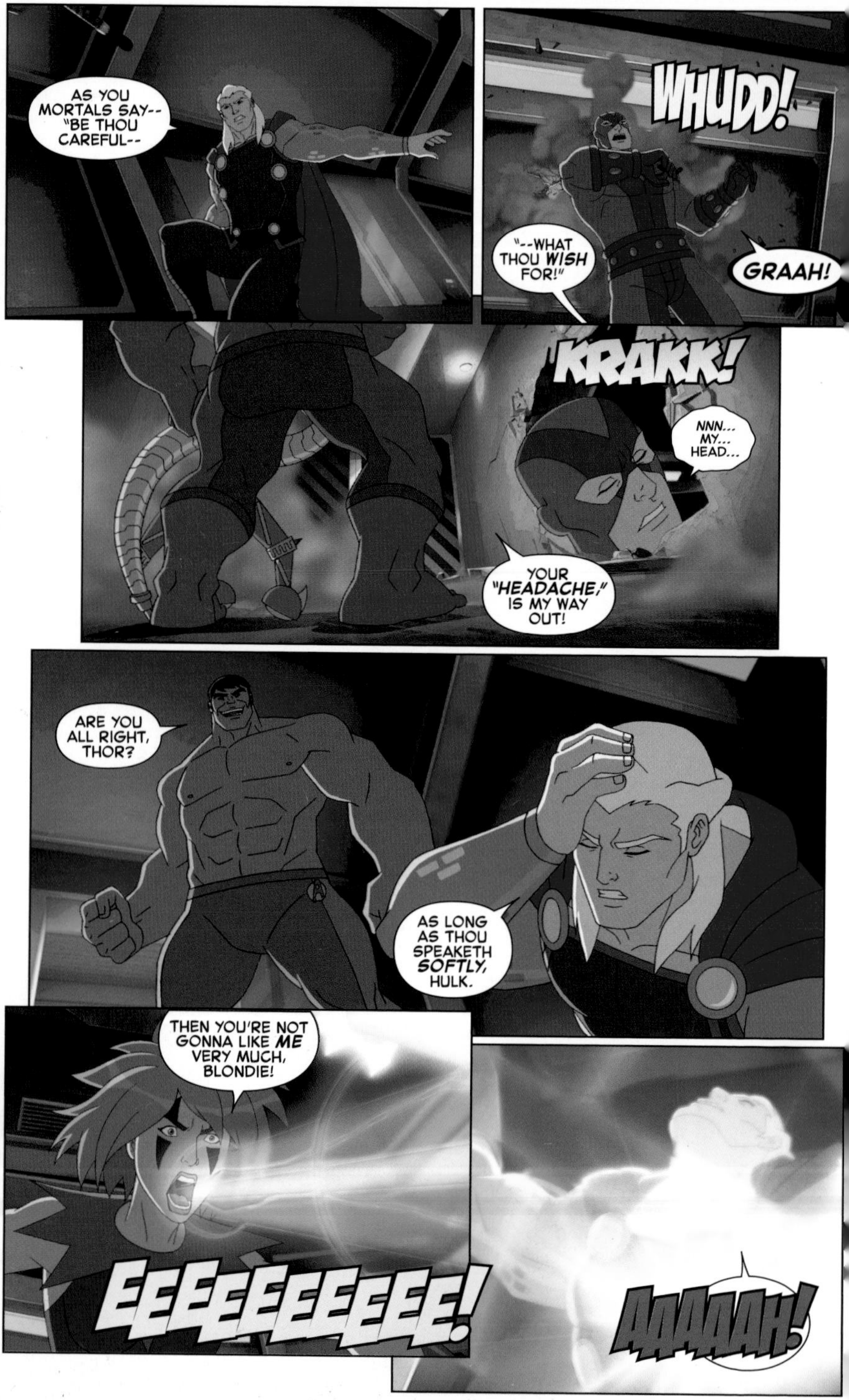
AS YOU MORTALS SAY-- "BE THOU CAREFUL--
WHUDD!
"--WHAT THOU WISH FOR!"
GRAAH!
KRAKK!
NNN... MY... HEAD...
YOUR "HEADACHE," IS MY WAY OUT!
ARE YOU ALL RIGHT, THOR?
AS LONG AS THOU SPEAKETH SOFTLY, HULK.
THEN YOU'RE NOT GONNA LIKE ME VERY MUCH, BLONDIE!
EEEEEEEEEEE!
AAAAAH!

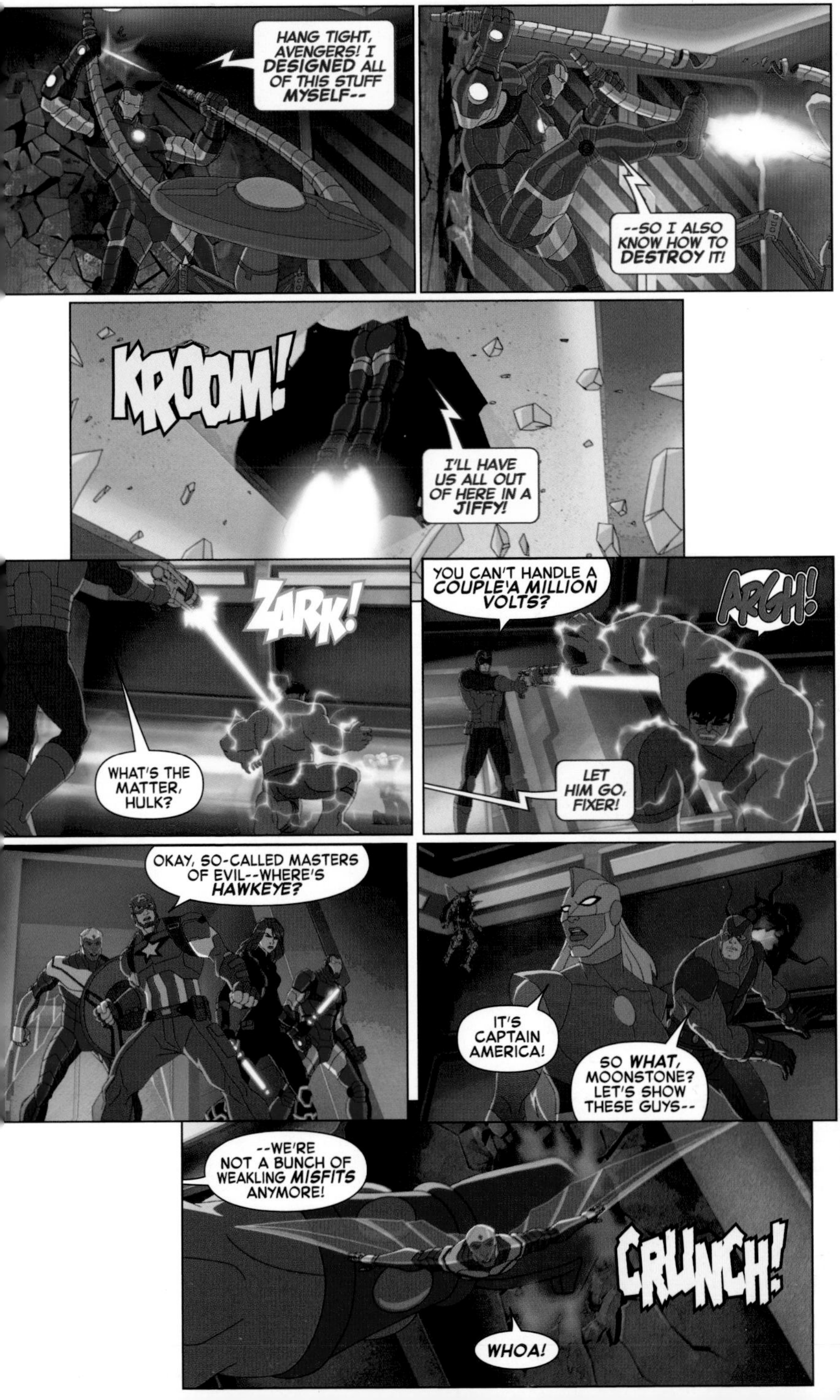
HANG TIGHT, AVENGERS! I DESIGNED ALL OF THIS STUFF MYSELF--
--SO I ALSO KNOW HOW TO DESTROY IT!
KROOM!
I'LL HAVE US ALL OUT OF HERE IN A JIFFY!
ZARK!
WHAT'S THE MATTER, HULK?
YOU CAN'T HANDLE A COUPLE'A MILLION VOLTS?
ARGH!
LET HIM GO, FIXER!
OKAY, SO-CALLED MASTERS OF EVIL--WHERE'S HAWKEYE?
IT'S CAPTAIN AMERICA!
SO WHAT, MOONSTONE? LET'S SHOW THESE GUYS--
--WE'RE NOT A BUNCH OF WEAKLING MISFITS ANYMORE!
CRUNCH!
WHOA!

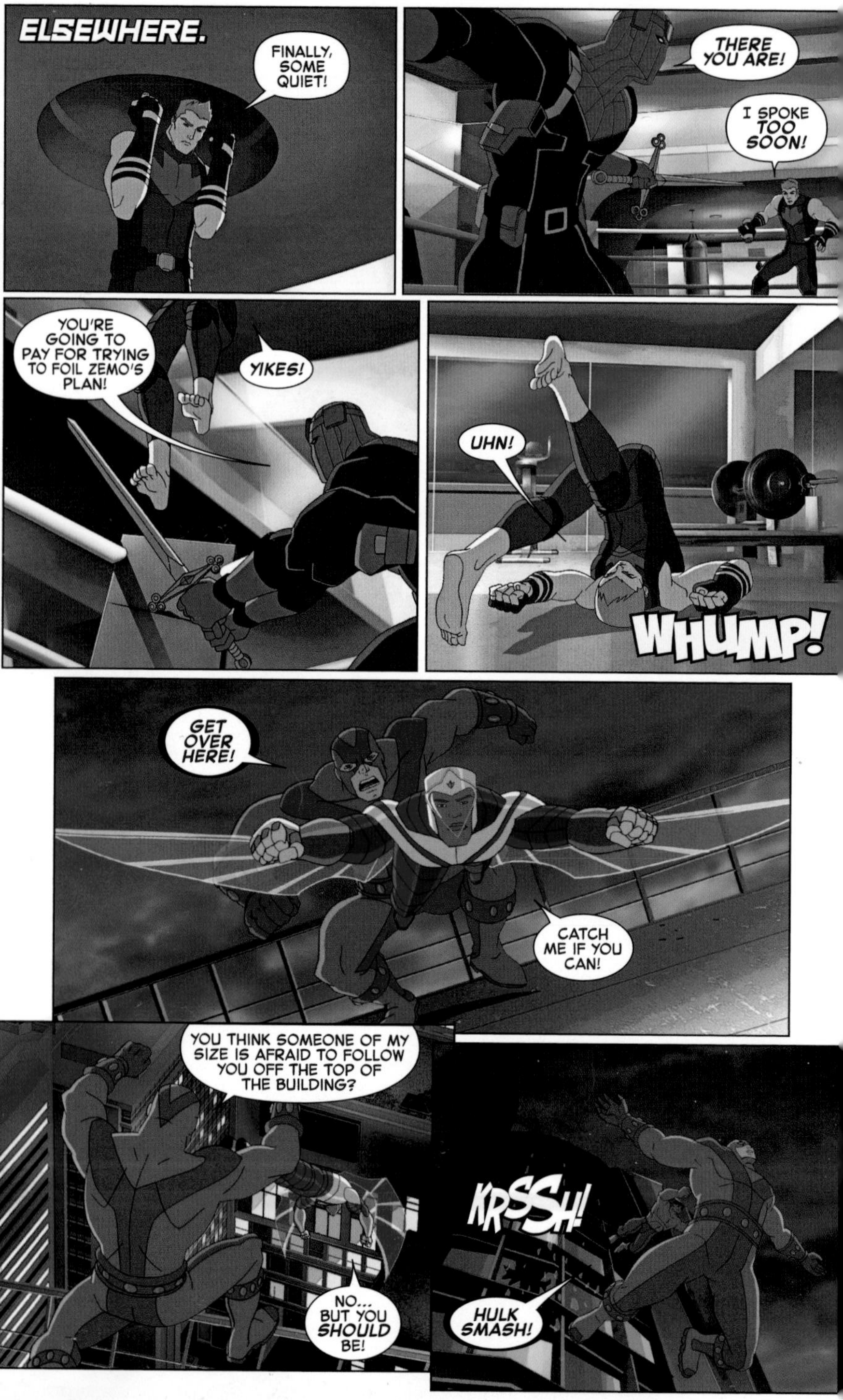

ELSEWHERE.
FINALLY, SOME QUIET!
THERE YOU ARE!
I SPOKE TOO SOON!
YOU'RE GOING TO PAY FOR TRYING TO FOIL ZEMO'S PLAN!
YIKES!
UHN!
WHUMP!
GET OVER HERE!
CATCH ME IF YOU CAN!
YOU THINK SOMEONE OF MY SIZE IS AFRAID TO FOLLOW YOU OFF THE TOP OF THE BUILDING?
NO... BUT YOU SHOULD BE!
KRSSH!
HULK SMASH!

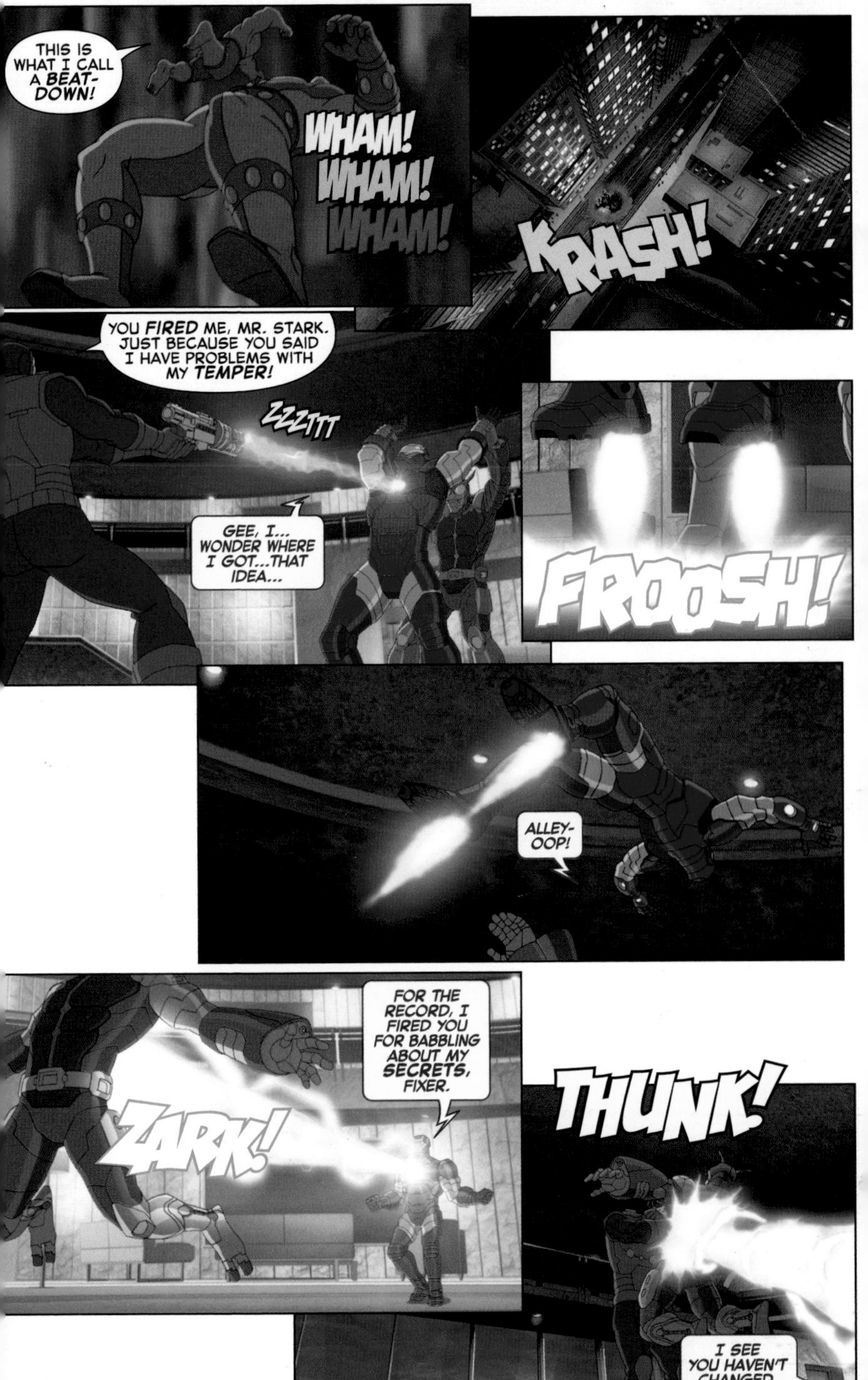
THIS IS WHAT I CALL A BEAT-DOWN!
WHAM! WHAM! WHAM!
KRASH!
YOU FIRED ME, MR. STARK. JUST BECAUSE YOU SAID I HAVE PROBLEMS WITH MY TEMPER!
ZZZTTT
GEE, I... WONDER WHERE I GOT...THAT IDEA...
FROOSH!
ALLEY-OOP!
FOR THE RECORD, I FIRED YOU FOR BABBLING ABOUT MY SECRETS, FIXER.
ZARK!
THUNK!
I SEE YOU HAVEN'T CHANGED.

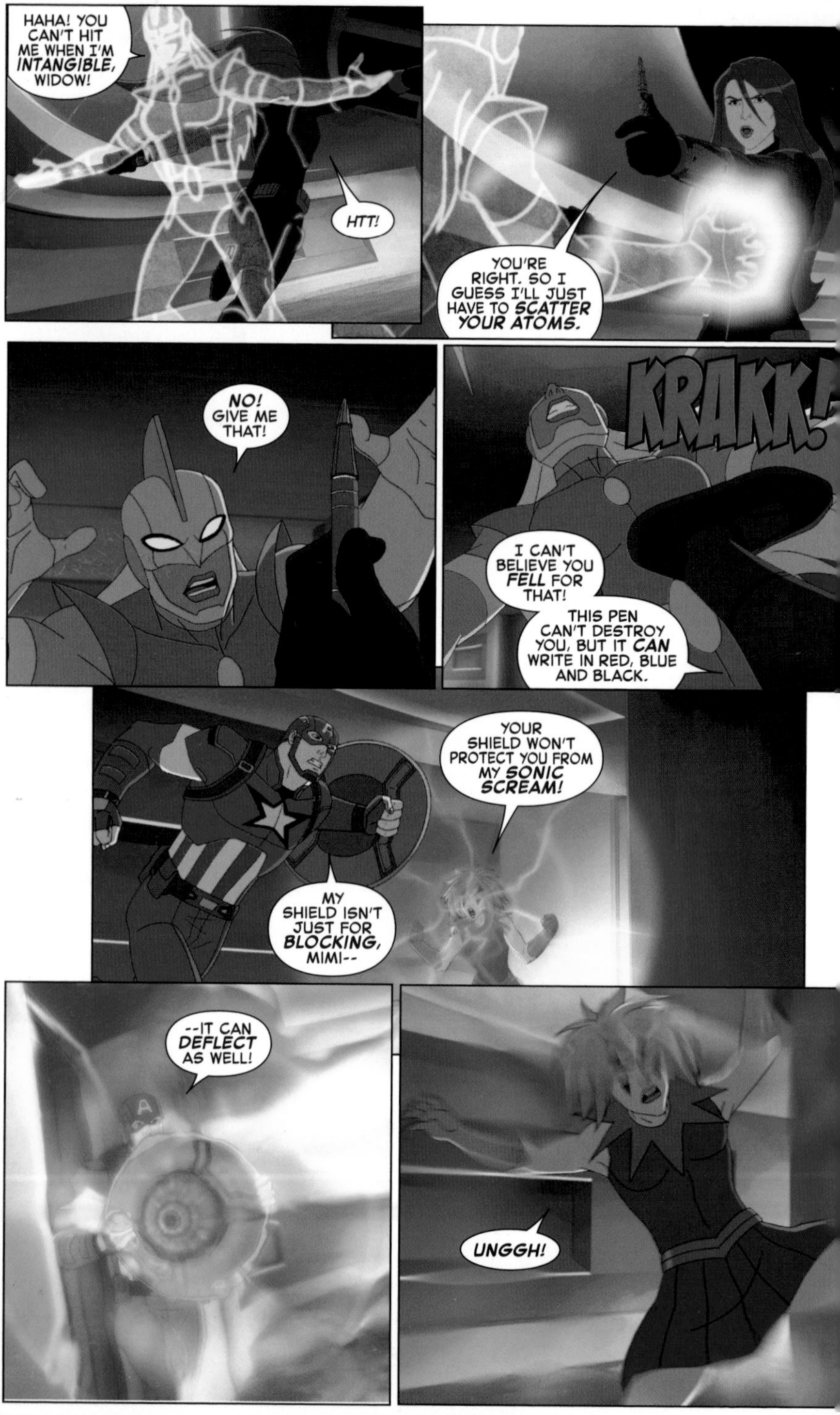
HAHA! YOU CAN'T HIT ME WHEN I'M *INTANGIBLE*, WIDOW!
HTT!
YOU'RE RIGHT. SO I GUESS I'LL JUST HAVE TO *SCATTER YOUR ATOMS.*
NO! GIVE ME THAT!
KRAKK!
I CAN'T BELIEVE YOU *FELL* FOR THAT!
THIS PEN CAN'T DESTROY YOU, BUT IT *CAN* WRITE IN RED, BLUE AND BLACK.
YOUR SHIELD WON'T PROTECT YOU FROM MY *SONIC SCREAM!*
MY SHIELD ISN'T JUST FOR *BLOCKING*, MIMI--
--IT CAN *DEFLECT* AS WELL!
UNGGH!

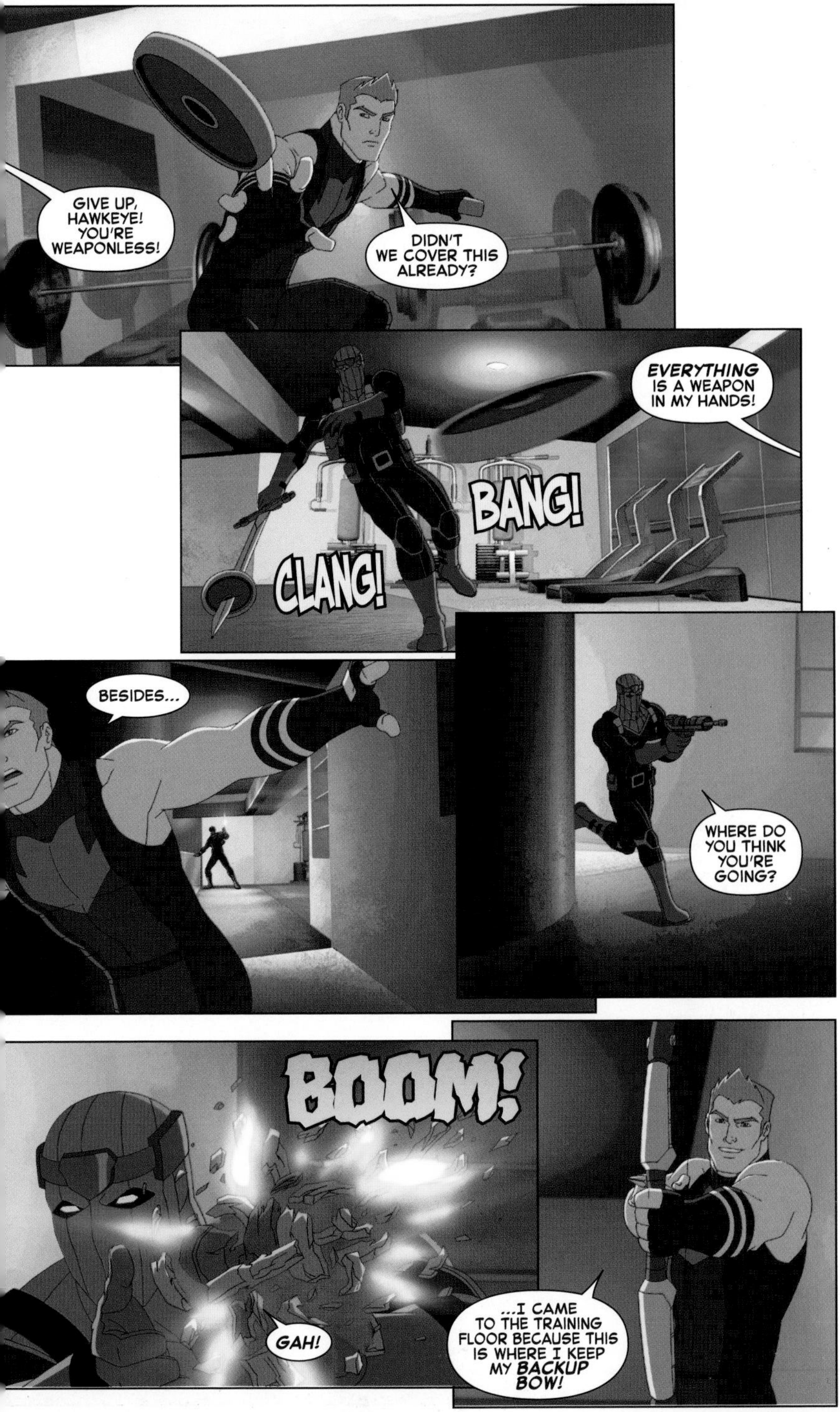

GIVE UP, HAWKEYE! YOU'RE WEAPONLESS!
DIDN'T WE COVER THIS ALREADY?
EVERYTHING IS A WEAPON IN MY HANDS!
BANG!
CLANG!
BESIDES...
WHERE DO YOU THINK YOU'RE GOING?
BOOM!
GAH!
...I CAME TO THE TRAINING FLOOR BECAUSE THIS IS WHERE I KEEP MY *BACKUP BOW!*

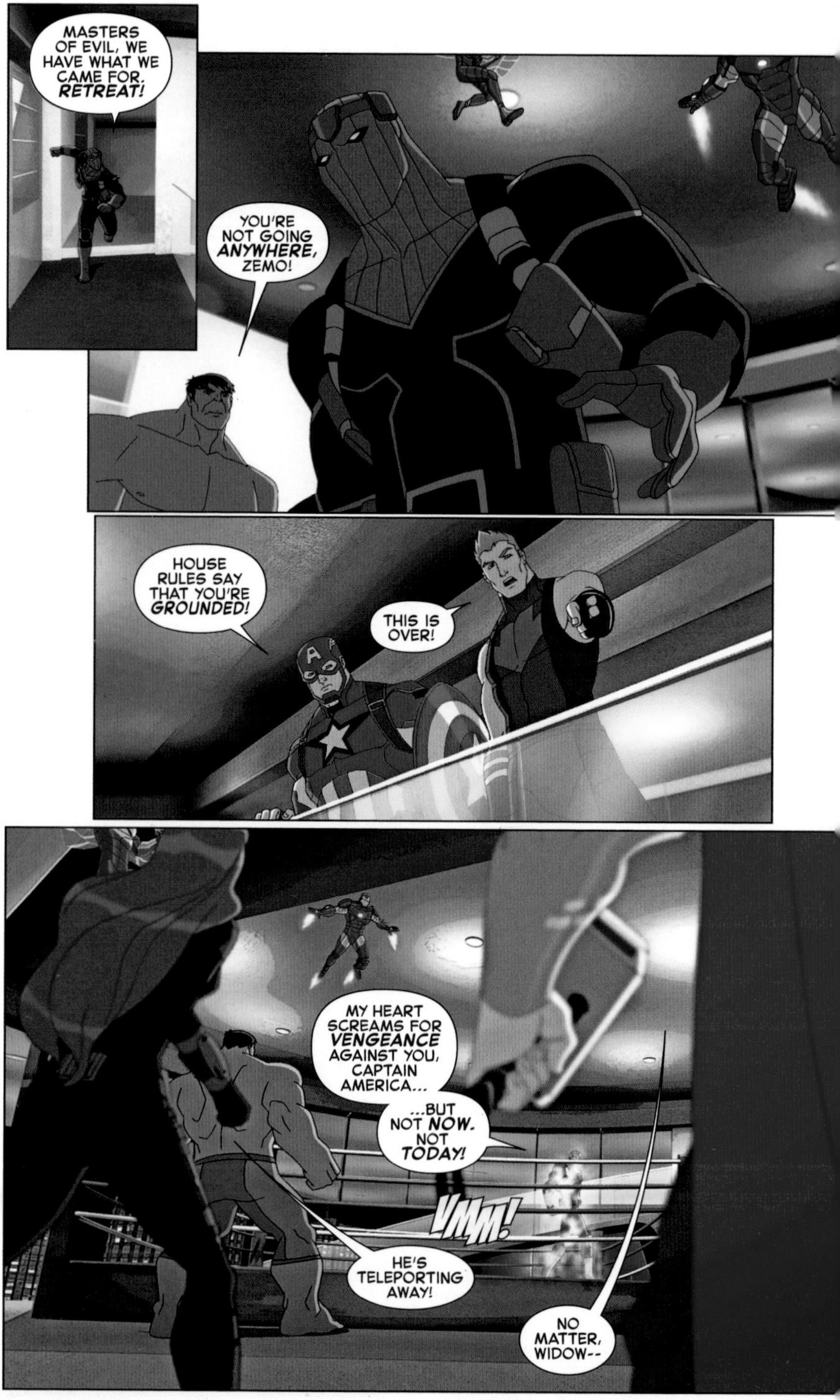
MASTERS OF EVIL, WE HAVE WHAT WE CAME FOR. *RETREAT!*
YOU'RE NOT GOING *ANYWHERE,* ZEMO!
HOUSE RULES SAY THAT YOU'RE *GROUNDED!*
THIS IS OVER!
MY HEART SCREAMS FOR *VENGEANCE* AGAINST YOU, CAPTAIN AMERICA...
...BUT NOT *NOW.* NOT *TODAY!*
VMM!
HE'S TELEPORTING AWAY!
NO MATTER, WIDOW--

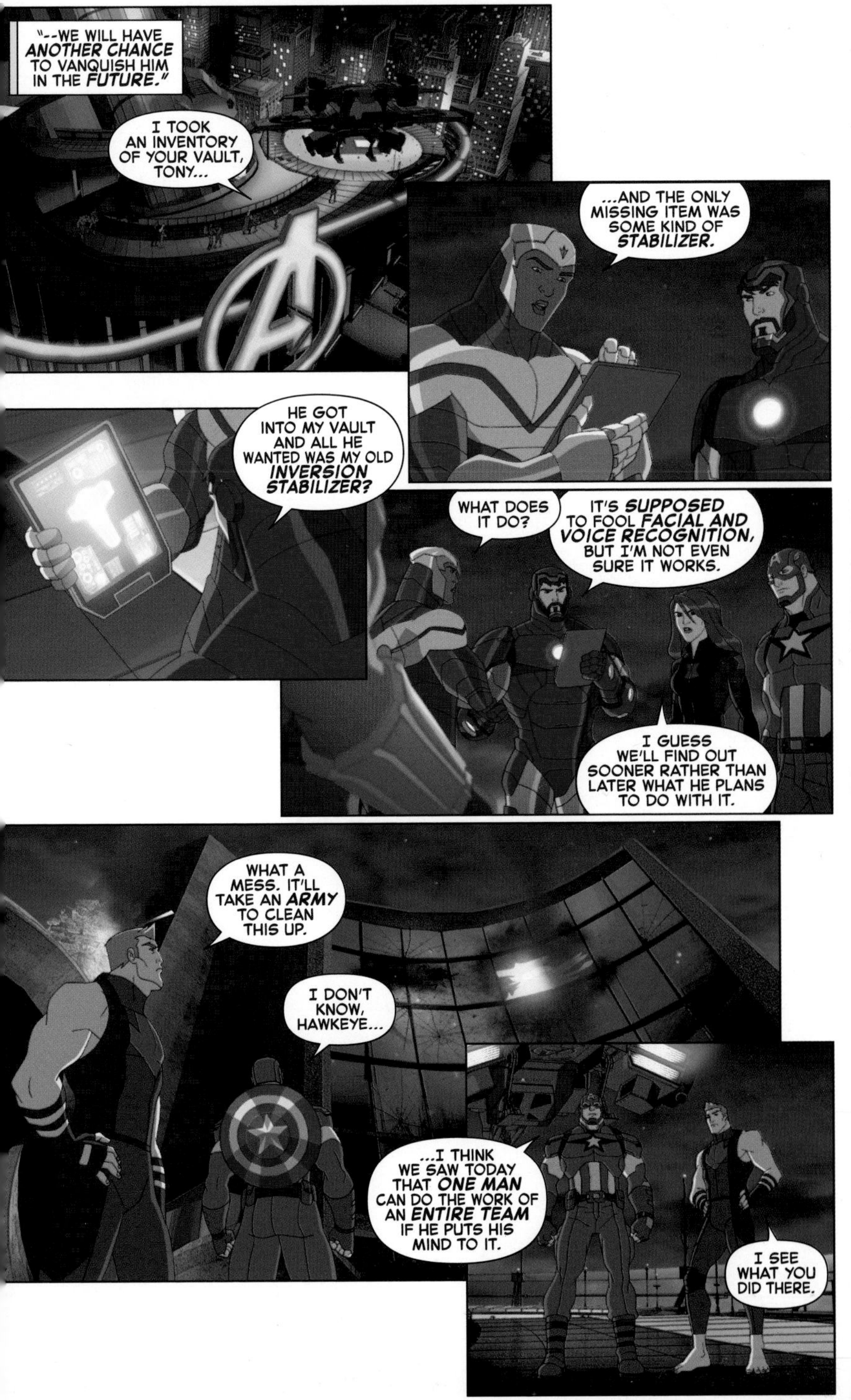
"--WE WILL HAVE ANOTHER CHANCE TO VANQUISH HIM IN THE FUTURE."
I TOOK AN INVENTORY OF YOUR VAULT, TONY...
...AND THE ONLY MISSING ITEM WAS SOME KIND OF STABILIZER.
HE GOT INTO MY VAULT AND ALL HE WANTED WAS MY OLD INVERSION STABILIZER?
WHAT DOES IT DO?
IT'S SUPPOSED TO FOOL FACIAL AND VOICE RECOGNITION, BUT I'M NOT EVEN SURE IT WORKS.
I GUESS WE'LL FIND OUT SOONER RATHER THAN LATER WHAT HE PLANS TO DO WITH IT.
WHAT A MESS. IT'LL TAKE AN ARMY TO CLEAN THIS UP.
I DON'T KNOW, HAWKEYE...
...I THINK WE SAW TODAY THAT ONE MAN CAN DO THE WORK OF AN ENTIRE TEAM IF HE PUTS HIS MIND TO IT.
I SEE WHAT YOU DID THERE.

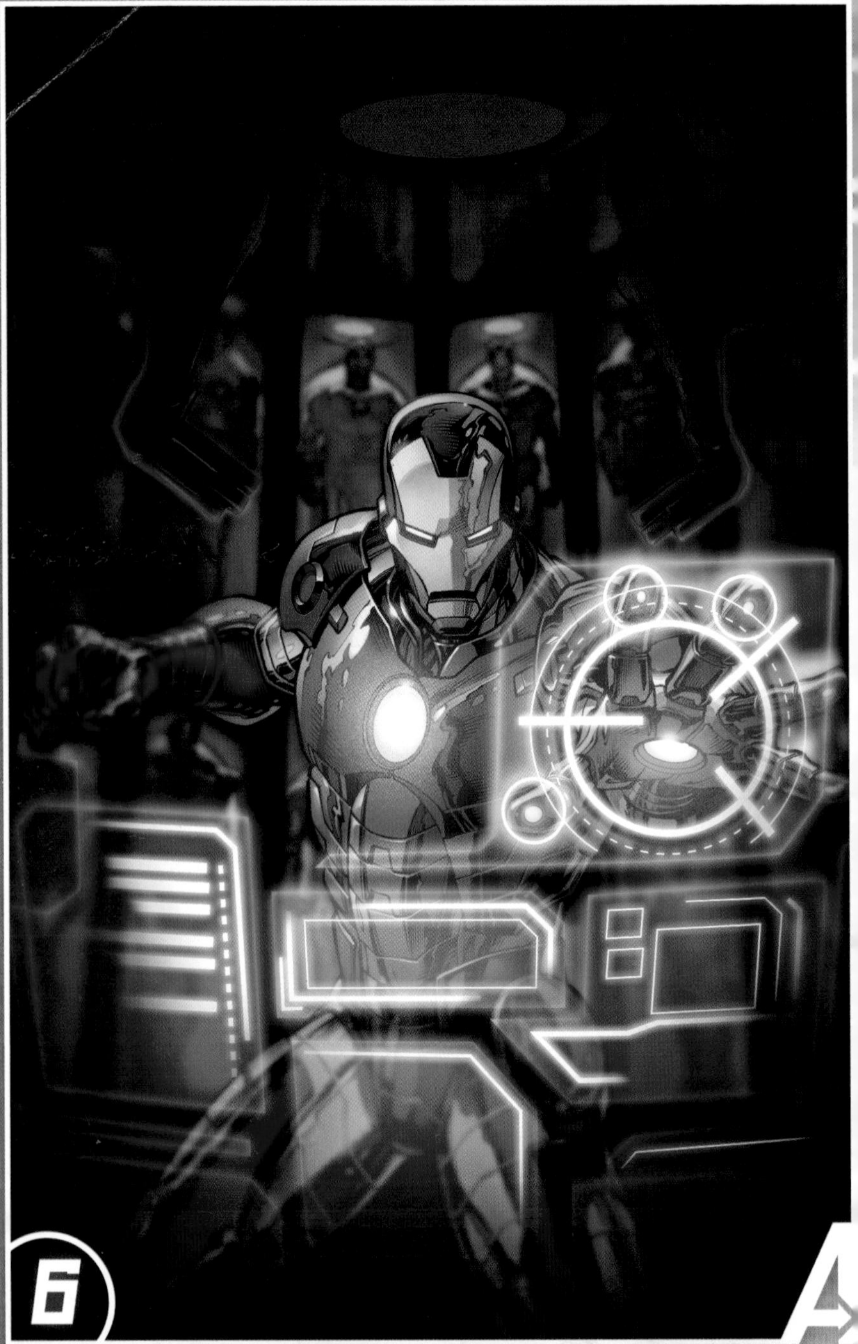
6

THE THUNDERBOLTS

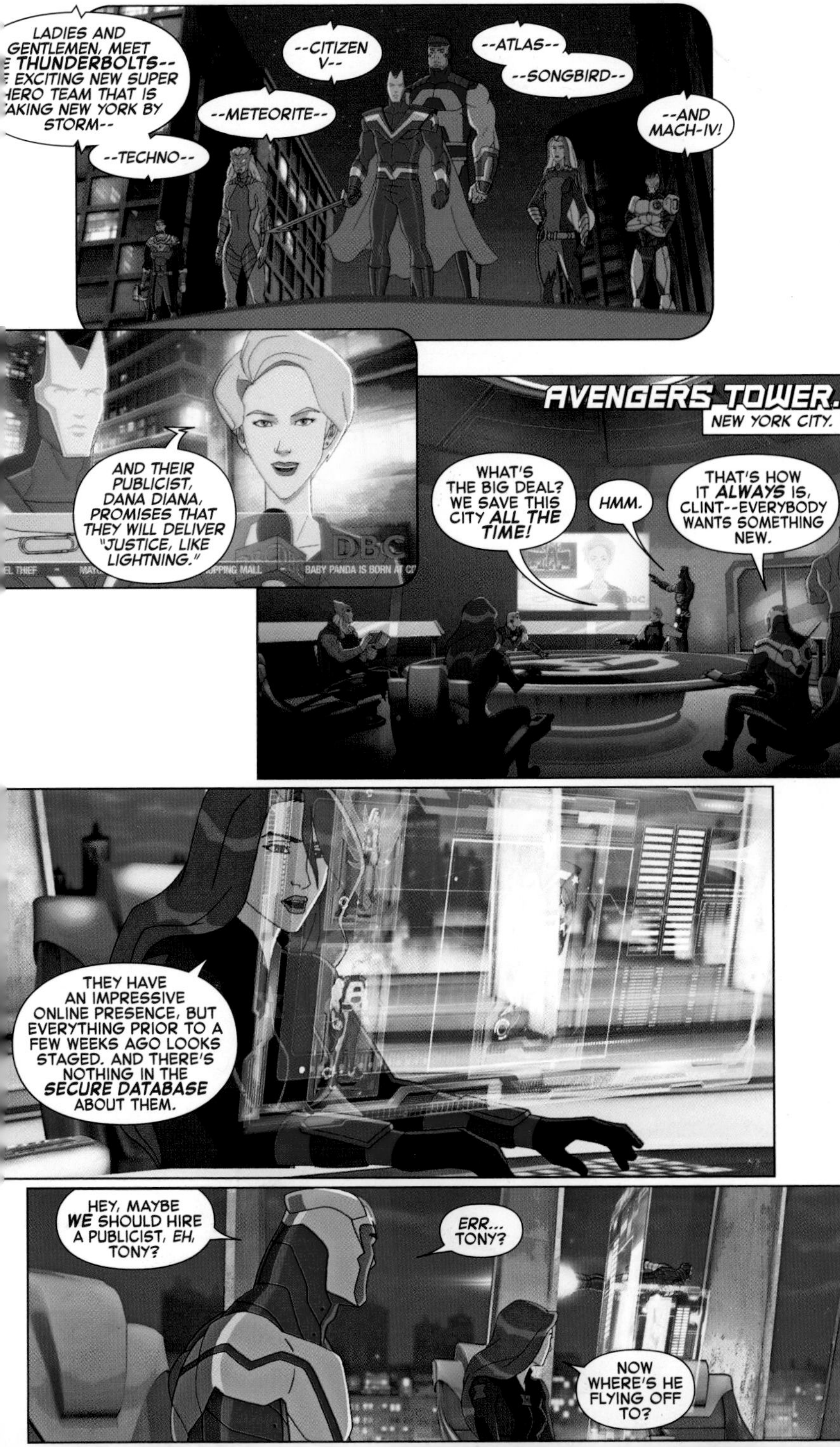

LADIES AND GENTLEMEN, MEET E THUNDERBOLTS-- E EXCITING NEW SUPER HERO TEAM THAT IS AKING NEW YORK BY STORM--
--TECHNO--
--METEORITE--
--CITIZEN V--
--ATLAS--
--SONGBIRD--
--AND MACH-IV!
AND THEIR PUBLICIST, DANA DIANA, PROMISES THAT THEY WILL DELIVER "JUSTICE, LIKE LIGHTNING."
DBC
BABY PANDA IS BORN AT CI
AVENGERS TOWER.
NEW YORK CITY.
WHAT'S THE BIG DEAL? WE SAVE THIS CITY ALL THE TIME!
HMM.
THAT'S HOW IT ALWAYS IS, CLINT--EVERYBODY WANTS SOMETHING NEW.
THEY HAVE AN IMPRESSIVE ONLINE PRESENCE, BUT EVERYTHING PRIOR TO A FEW WEEKS AGO LOOKS STAGED. AND THERE'S NOTHING IN THE SECURE DATABASE ABOUT THEM.
HEY, MAYBE WE SHOULD HIRE A PUBLICIST, EH, TONY?
ERR... TONY?
NOW WHERE'S HE FLYING OFF TO?

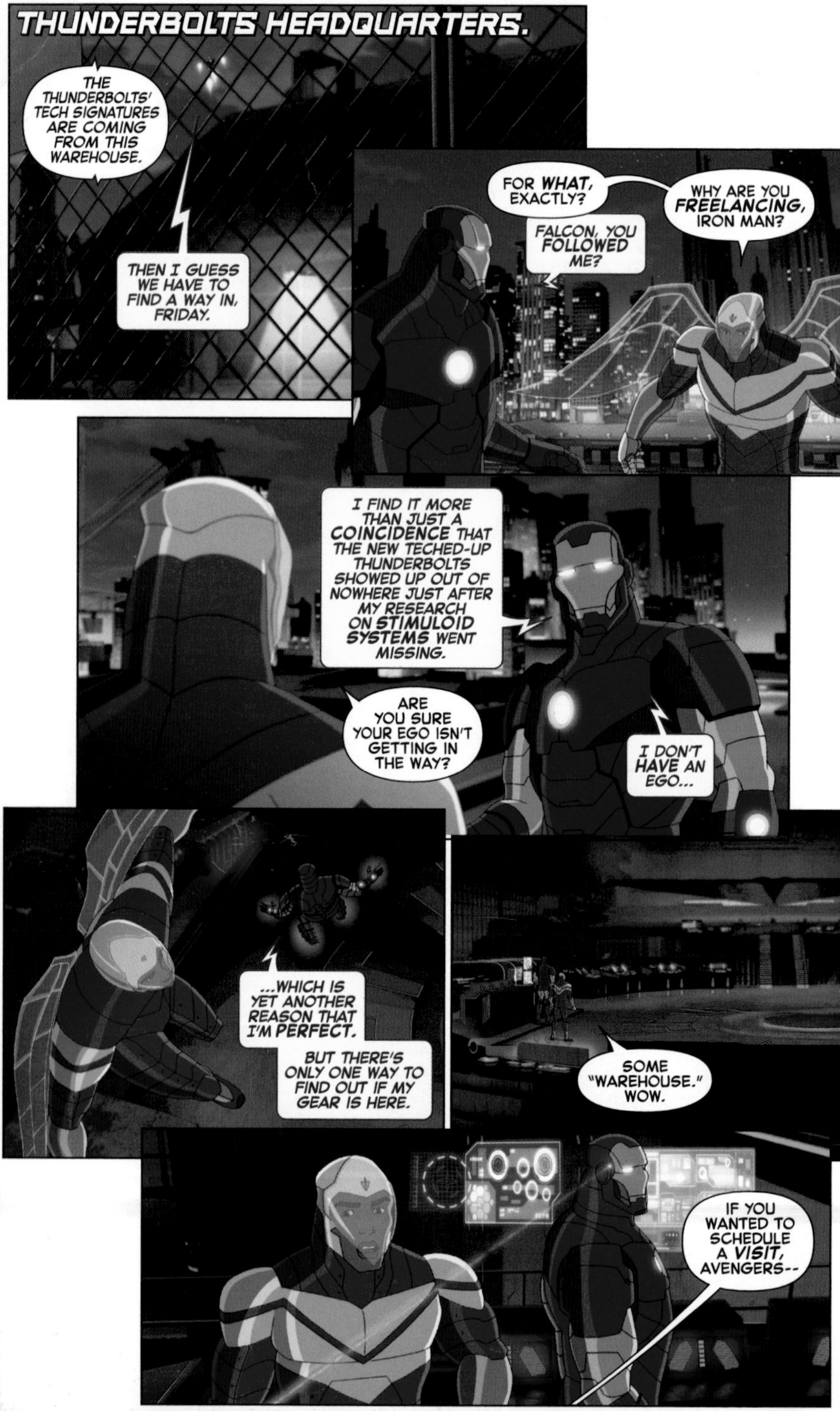
THUNDERBOLTS HEADQUARTERS.
THE THUNDERBOLTS' TECH SIGNATURES ARE COMING FROM THIS WAREHOUSE.
THEN I GUESS WE HAVE TO FIND A WAY IN, FRIDAY.
WHY ARE YOU FREELANCING, IRON MAN?
FOR WHAT, EXACTLY?
FALCON, YOU FOLLOWED ME?
I FIND IT MORE THAN JUST A COINCIDENCE THAT THE NEW TECHED-UP THUNDERBOLTS SHOWED UP OUT OF NOWHERE JUST AFTER MY RESEARCH ON STIMULOID SYSTEMS WENT MISSING.
ARE YOU SURE YOUR EGO ISN'T GETTING IN THE WAY?
I DON'T HAVE AN EGO...
...WHICH IS YET ANOTHER REASON THAT I'M PERFECT.
BUT THERE'S ONLY ONE WAY TO FIND OUT IF MY GEAR IS HERE.
SOME "WAREHOUSE." WOW.
IF YOU WANTED TO SCHEDULE A VISIT, AVENGERS--

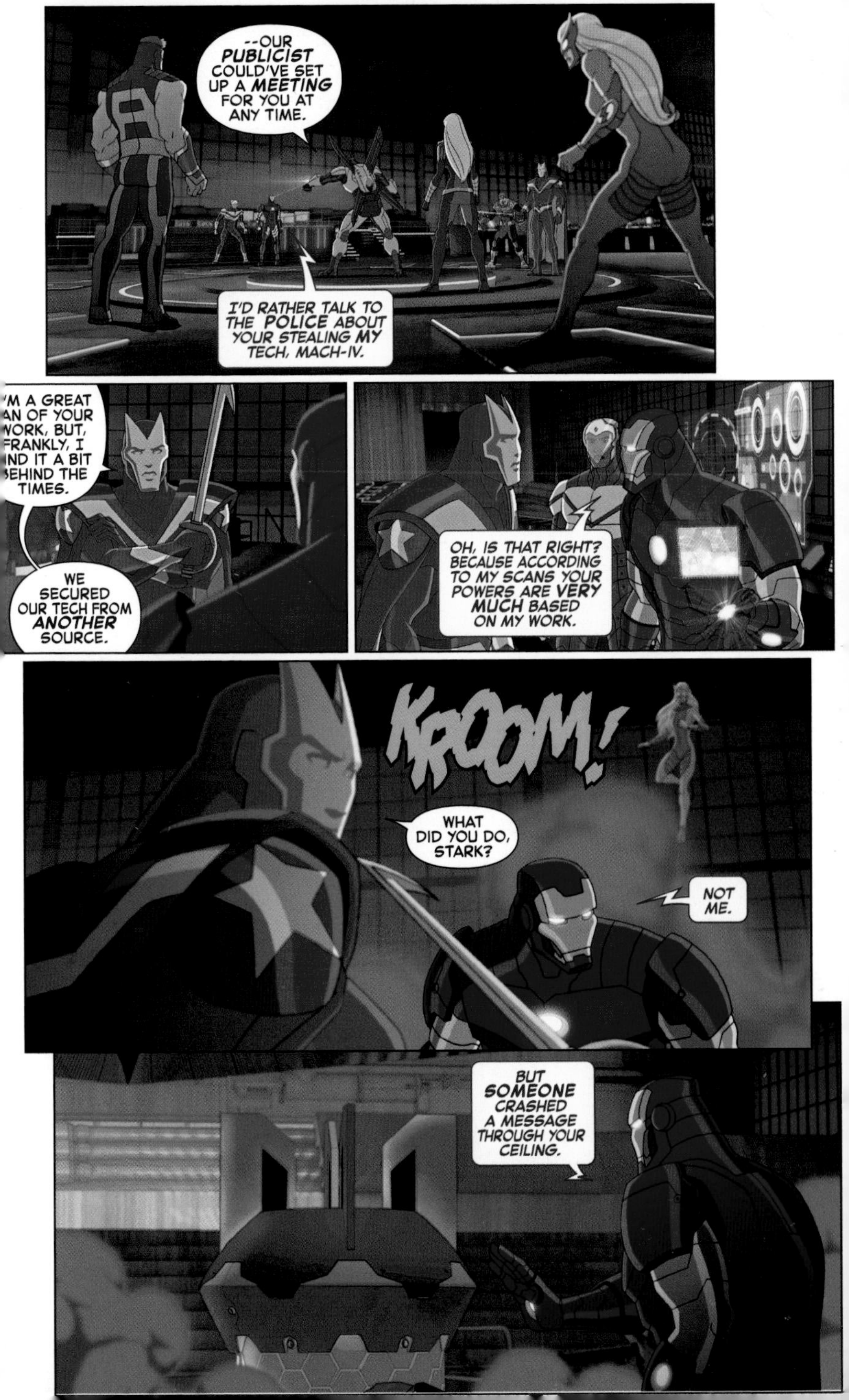
--OUR PUBLICIST COULD'VE SET UP A MEETING FOR YOU AT ANY TIME.
I'D RATHER TALK TO THE POLICE ABOUT YOUR STEALING MY TECH, MACH-IV.
'M A GREAT AN OF YOUR WORK, BUT, FRANKLY, I ND IT A BIT BEHIND THE TIMES.
WE SECURED OUR TECH FROM ANOTHER SOURCE.
OH, IS THAT RIGHT? BECAUSE ACCORDING TO MY SCANS YOUR POWERS ARE VERY MUCH BASED ON MY WORK.
KROOM!
WHAT DID YOU DO, STARK?
NOT ME.
BUT SOMEONE CRASHED A MESSAGE THROUGH YOUR CEILING.

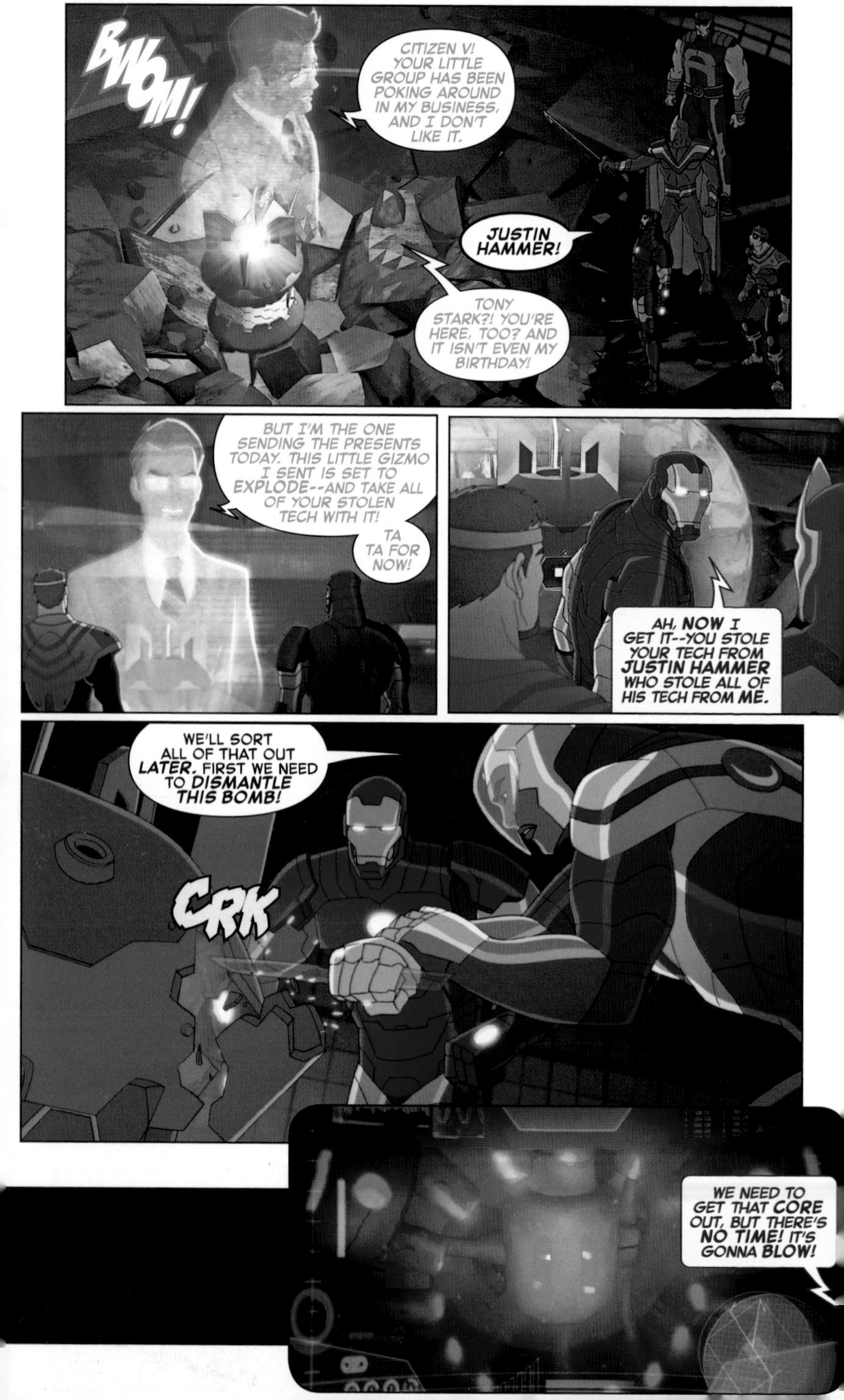

BWOM!
CITIZEN V! YOUR LITTLE GROUP HAS BEEN POKING AROUND IN MY BUSINESS, AND I DON'T LIKE IT.
JUSTIN HAMMER!
TONY STARK?! YOU'RE HERE, TOO? AND IT ISN'T EVEN MY BIRTHDAY!
BUT I'M THE ONE SENDING THE PRESENTS TODAY. THIS LITTLE GIZMO I SENT IS SET TO EXPLODE--AND TAKE ALL OF YOUR STOLEN TECH WITH IT!
TA TA FOR NOW!
AH, NOW I GET IT--YOU STOLE YOUR TECH FROM JUSTIN HAMMER WHO STOLE ALL OF HIS TECH FROM ME.
WE'LL SORT ALL OF THAT OUT LATER. FIRST WE NEED TO DISMANTLE THIS BOMB!
CRK
WE NEED TO GET THAT CORE OUT, BUT THERE'S NO TIME! IT'S GONNA BLOW!

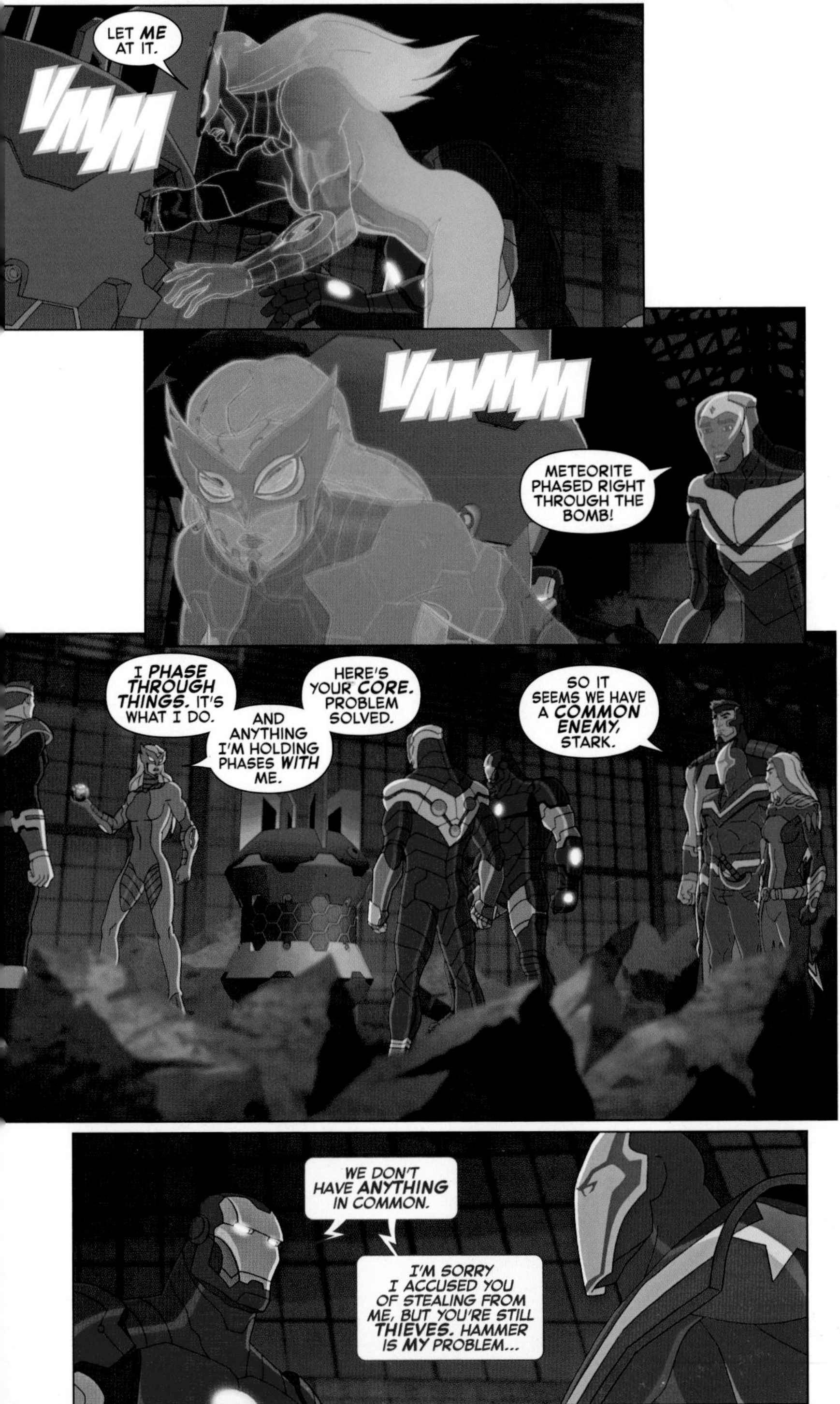
LET ME AT IT.
VMM
VMMM
METEORITE PHASED RIGHT THROUGH THE BOMB!
I PHASE THROUGH THINGS. IT'S WHAT I DO.
AND ANYTHING I'M HOLDING PHASES WITH ME.
HERE'S YOUR CORE. PROBLEM SOLVED.
SO IT SEEMS WE HAVE A COMMON ENEMY, STARK.
WE DON'T HAVE ANYTHING IN COMMON.
I'M SORRY I ACCUSED YOU OF STEALING FROM ME, BUT YOU'RE STILL THIEVES. HAMMER IS MY PROBLEM...

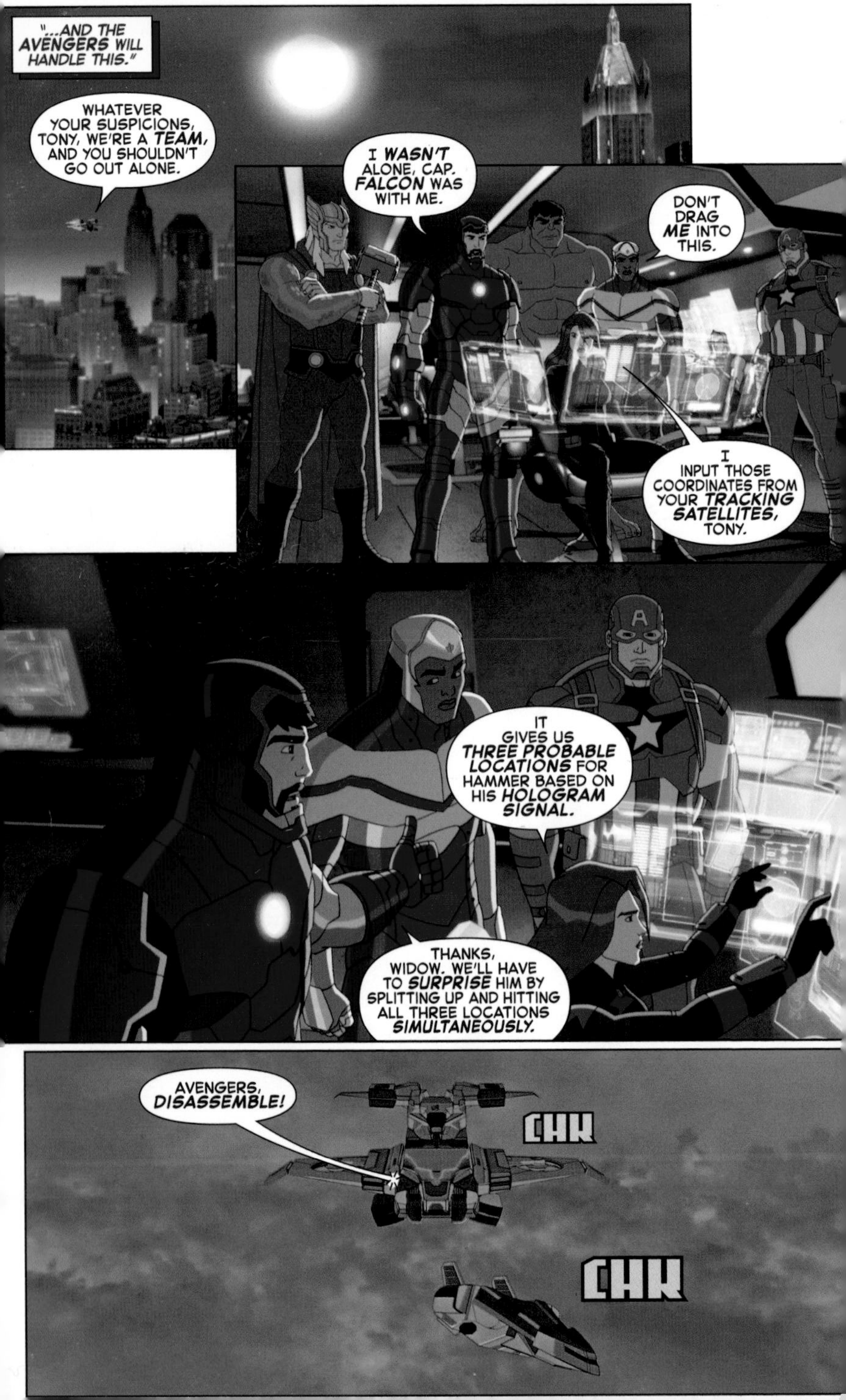
"...AND THE AVENGERS WILL HANDLE THIS."
WHATEVER YOUR SUSPICIONS, TONY, WE'RE A TEAM, AND YOU SHOULDN'T GO OUT ALONE.
I WASN'T ALONE, CAP. FALCON WAS WITH ME.
DON'T DRAG ME INTO THIS.
I INPUT THOSE COORDINATES FROM YOUR TRACKING SATELLITES, TONY.
IT GIVES US THREE PROBABLE LOCATIONS FOR HAMMER BASED ON HIS HOLOGRAM SIGNAL.
THANKS, WIDOW. WE'LL HAVE TO SURPRISE HIM BY SPLITTING UP AND HITTING ALL THREE LOCATIONS SIMULTANEOUSLY.
AVENGERS, DISASSEMBLE!
CHK
CHK

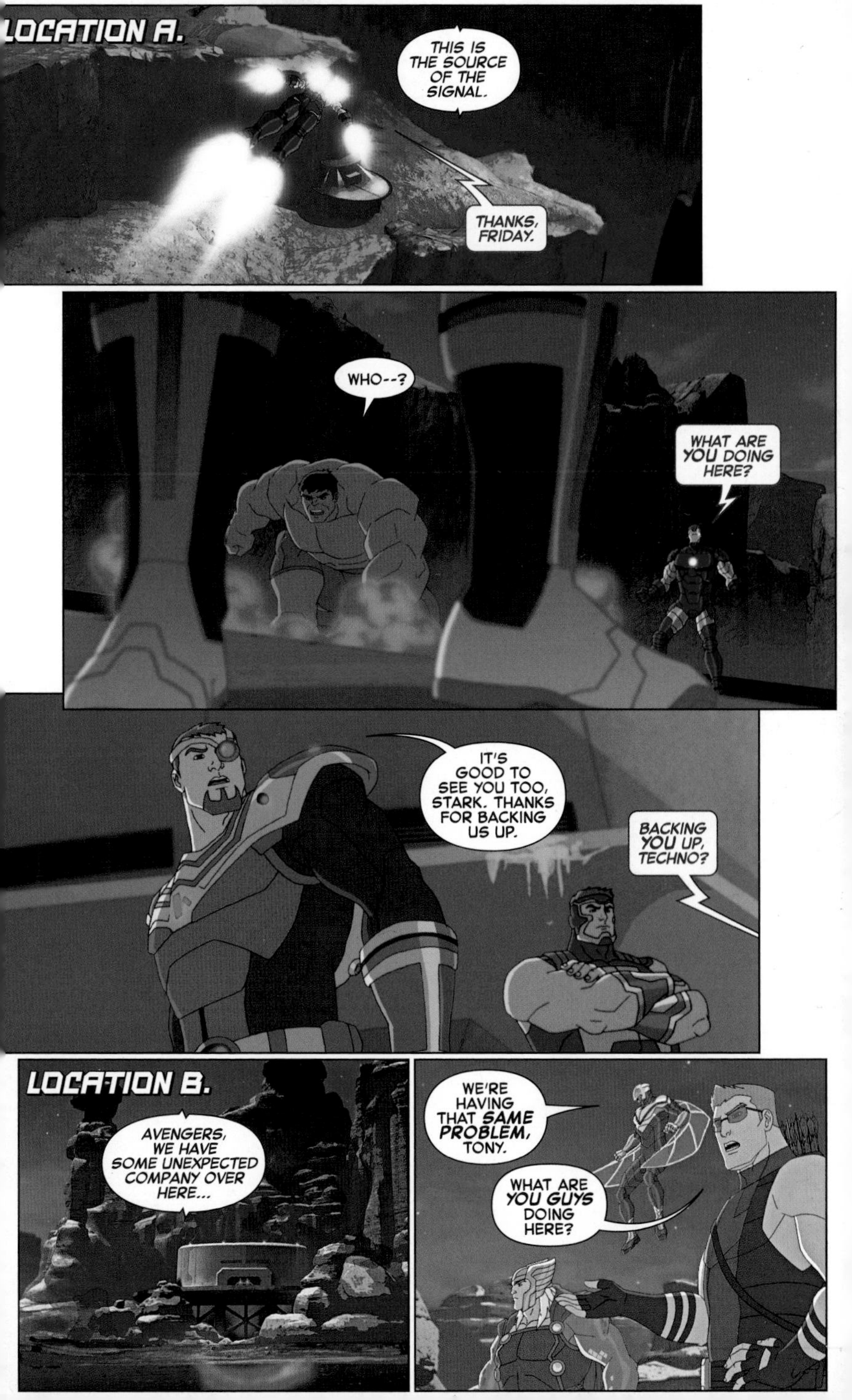
LOCATION A.
THIS IS THE SOURCE OF THE SIGNAL.
THANKS, FRIDAY.
WHO--?
WHAT ARE YOU DOING HERE?
IT'S GOOD TO SEE YOU TOO, STARK. THANKS FOR BACKING US UP.
BACKING YOU UP, TECHNO?
LOCATION B.
AVENGERS, WE HAVE SOME UNEXPECTED COMPANY OVER HERE...
WE'RE HAVING THAT SAME PROBLEM, TONY.
WHAT ARE YOU GUYS DOING HERE?

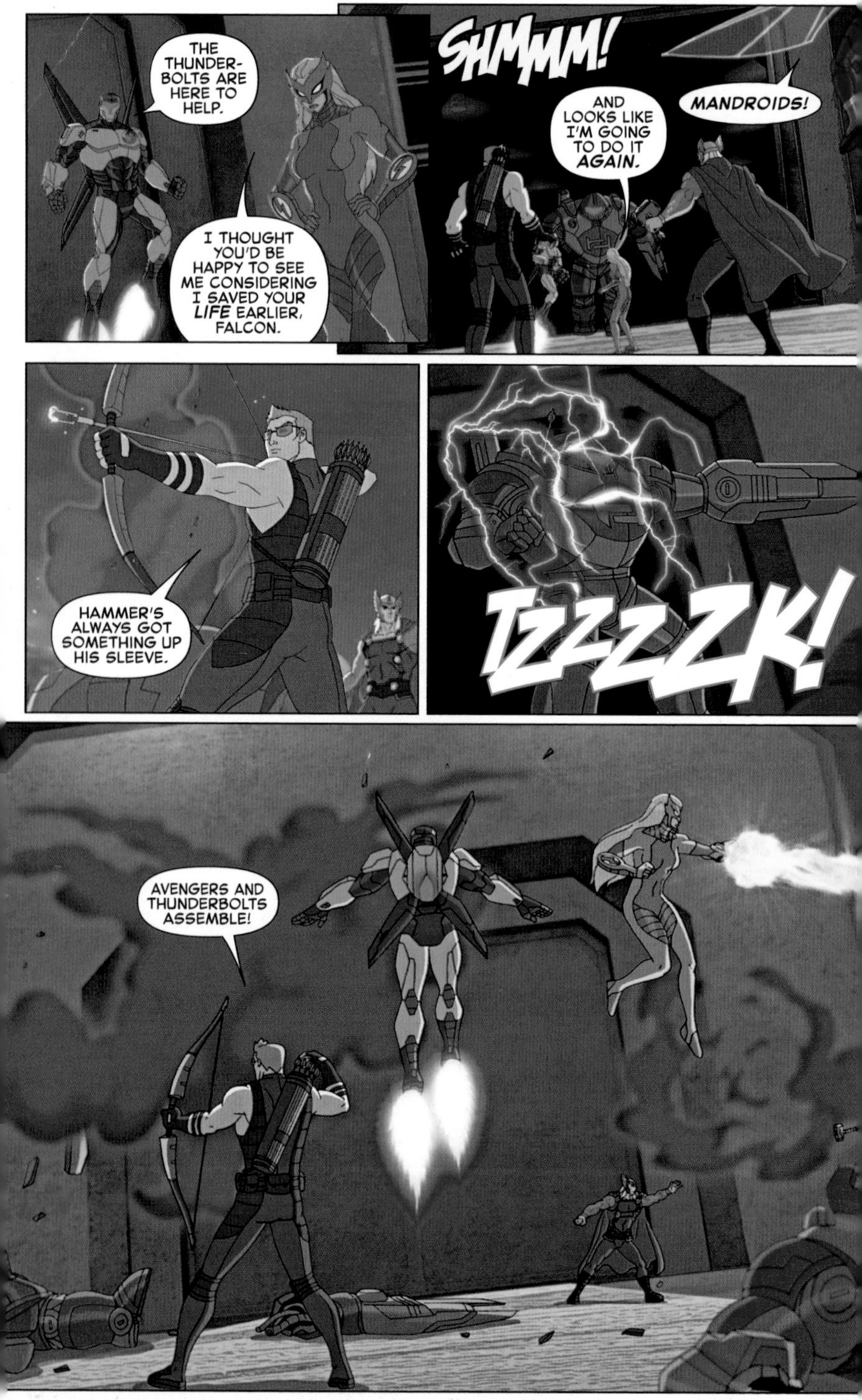
THE THUNDER-BOLTS ARE HERE TO HELP.
I THOUGHT YOU'D BE HAPPY TO SEE ME CONSIDERING I SAVED YOUR LIFE EARLIER, FALCON.
SHMMM!
AND LOOKS LIKE I'M GOING TO DO IT AGAIN.
MANDROIDS!
HAMMER'S ALWAYS GOT SOMETHING UP HIS SLEEVE.
TZZZZK!
AVENGERS AND THUNDERBOLTS ASSEMBLE!

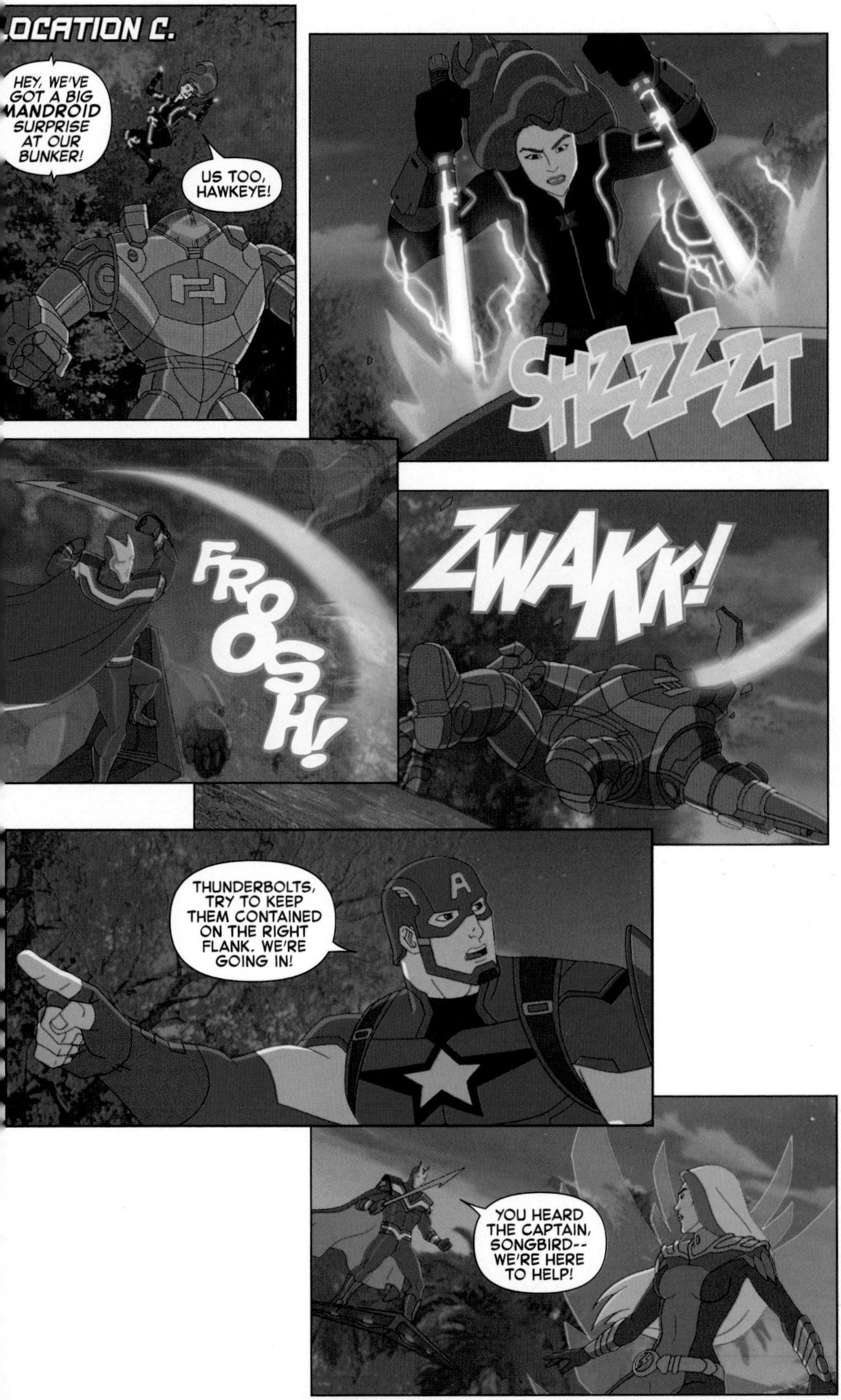

LOCATION C.
HEY, WE'VE GOT A BIG MANDROID SURPRISE AT OUR BUNKER!
US TOO, HAWKEYE!
SHZZZZT
FROOSH!
ZWAKK!
THUNDERBOLTS, TRY TO KEEP THEM CONTAINED ON THE RIGHT FLANK. WE'RE GOING IN!
YOU HEARD THE CAPTAIN, SONGBIRD-- WE'RE HERE TO HELP!

LOCATION A.

FRSH!

FRSH!

FRSH!

BRKOOM!

ROARR!

SHR///////P

AVENGERS,
WE'VE DEALT WITH
THE MANDROIDS
ON OUR SITE.

SCAN THE
BUNKERS FOR
TRAPS, THEN
GO IN.

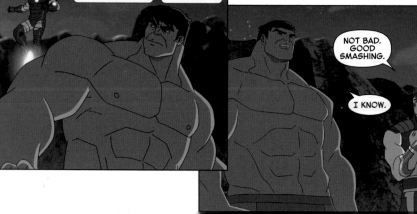

NOT BAD.
GOOD
SMASHING.

I KNOW.

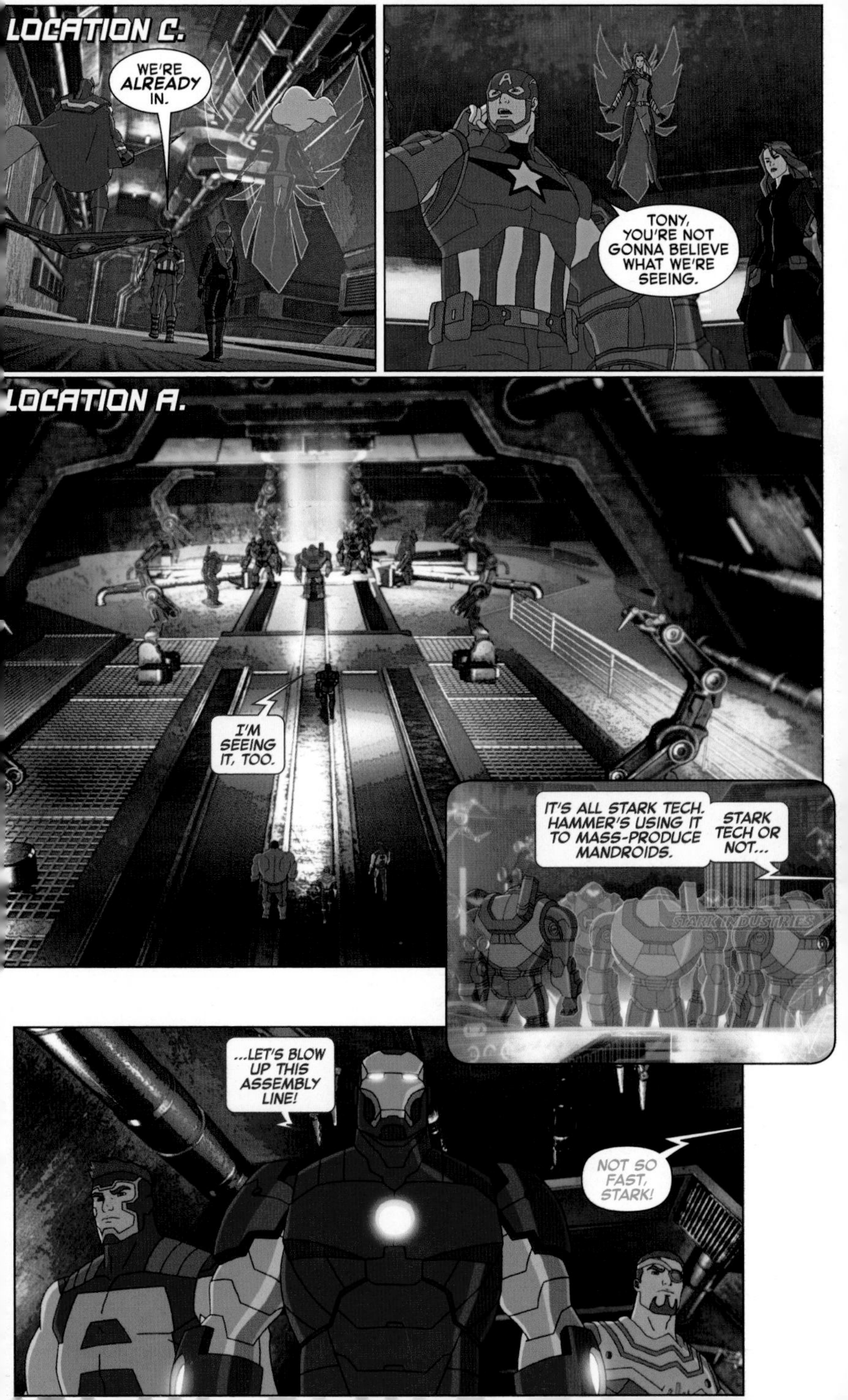
LOCATION C.
WE'RE ALREADY IN.
TONY, YOU'RE NOT GONNA BELIEVE WHAT WE'RE SEEING.
LOCATION A.
I'M SEEING IT, TOO.
IT'S ALL STARK TECH. HAMMER'S USING IT TO MASS-PRODUCE MANDROIDS.
STARK TECH OR NOT...
STARK INDUSTRIES
...LET'S BLOW UP THIS ASSEMBLY LINE!
NOT SO FAST, STARK!

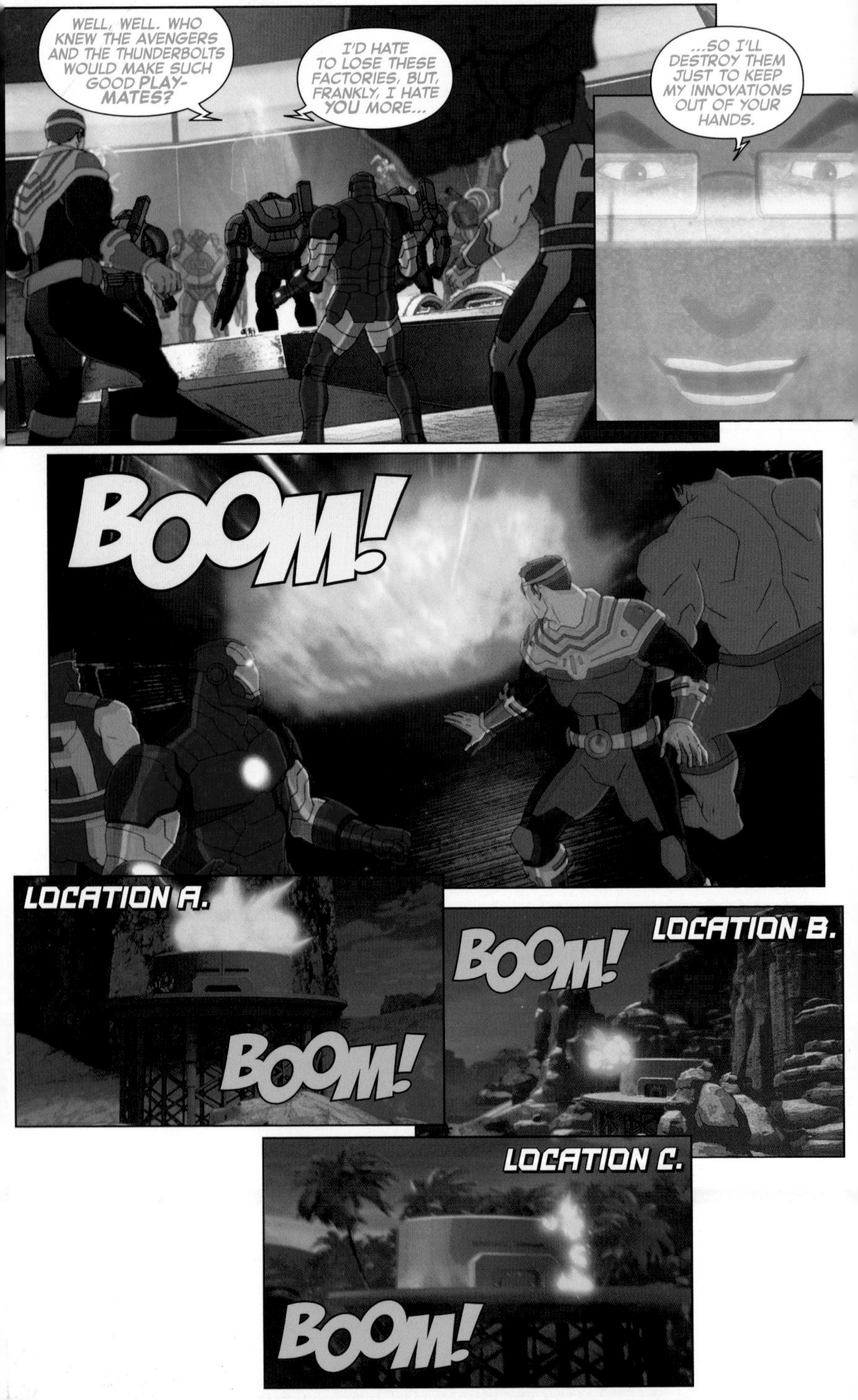
WELL, WELL. WHO KNEW THE AVENGERS AND THE THUNDERBOLTS WOULD MAKE SUCH GOOD PLAY-MATES?
I'D HATE TO LOSE THESE FACTORIES, BUT, FRANKLY, I HATE YOU MORE...
...SO I'LL DESTROY THEM JUST TO KEEP MY INNOVATIONS OUT OF YOUR HANDS.
BOOM!
LOCATION A.
BOOM!
BOOM!
LOCATION B.
LOCATION C.
BOOM!

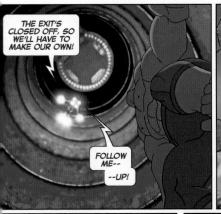

THE EXIT'S CLOSED OFF, SO WE'LL HAVE TO MAKE OUR OWN!

FOLLOW ME--

--UP!

BRKOOM!

IS EVERYONE OUT?

WE'RE OKAY, BUT FAR FROM HAPPY, TONY.

DO YOU HAVE A *REAL* LOCATION ON HAMMER?

I MAY HAVE SOME INFORMATION IN THAT REGARD.

IT SEEMS OUR PUBLICIST HAS BEEN DOING DOUBLE DUTY. OBSERVE.

JUST SAYING, MR. HAMMER, THAT IF YOU WANT TO KNOW WHERE THE *THUNDERBOLTS'* HEADQUARTERS IS, I MIGHT BE ABLE TO PROVIDE YOU WITH THAT INFORMATION... FOR A *PRICE.*

I'LL COMBINE MY SIGNAL TRACKING WITH YOUR VIDEO CALL SOURCE INFORMATION, CITIZEN V, AND...

I FOUND HIM!

I AM GOOD.

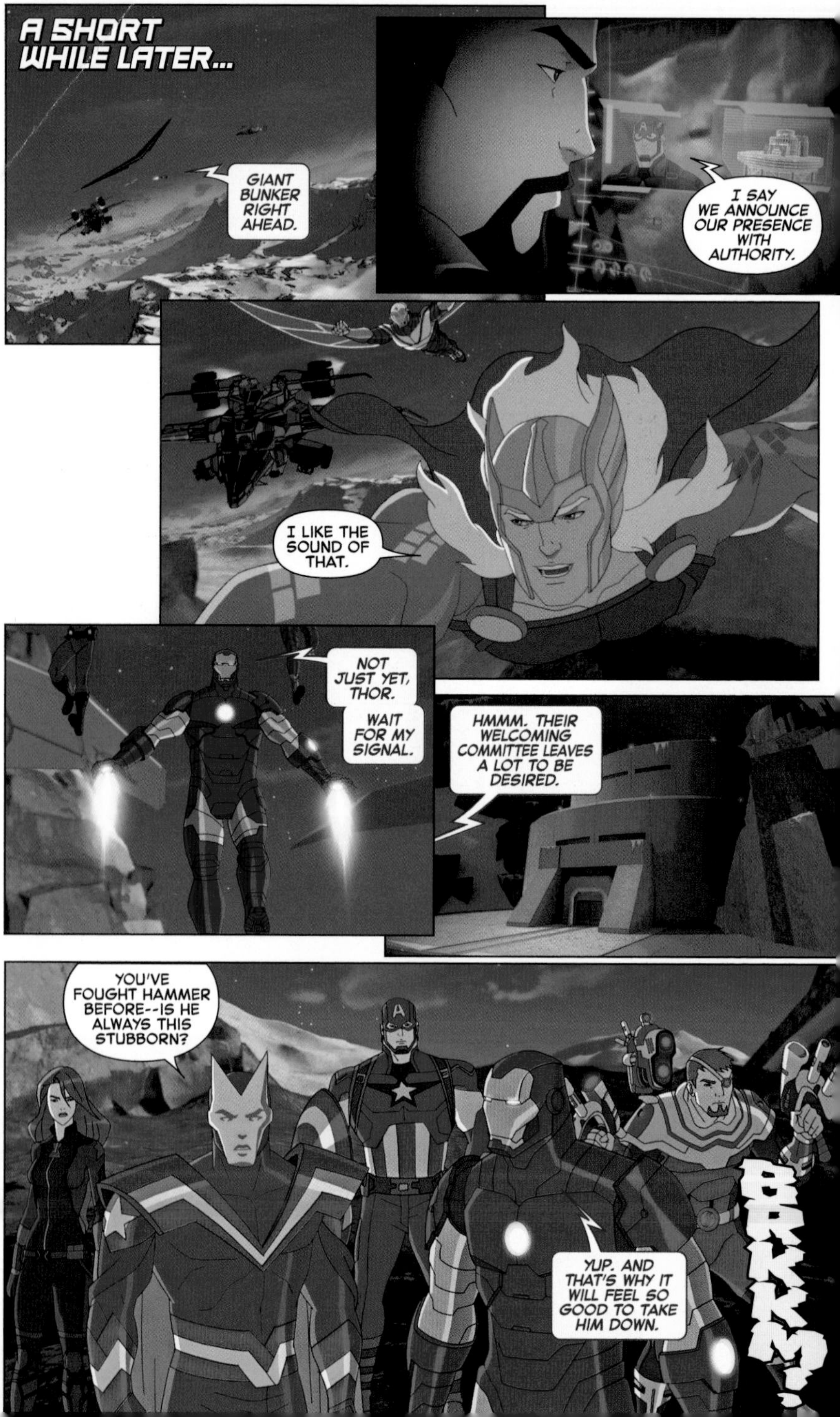
A SHORT WHILE LATER...
GIANT BUNKER RIGHT AHEAD.
I SAY WE ANNOUNCE OUR PRESENCE WITH AUTHORITY.
I LIKE THE SOUND OF THAT.
NOT JUST YET, THOR.
WAIT FOR MY SIGNAL.
HMMM. THEIR WELCOMING COMMITTEE LEAVES A LOT TO BE DESIRED.
YOU'VE FOUGHT HAMMER BEFORE--IS HE ALWAYS THIS STUBBORN?
YUP. AND THAT'S WHY IT WILL FEEL SO GOOD TO TAKE HIM DOWN.
BRKM!

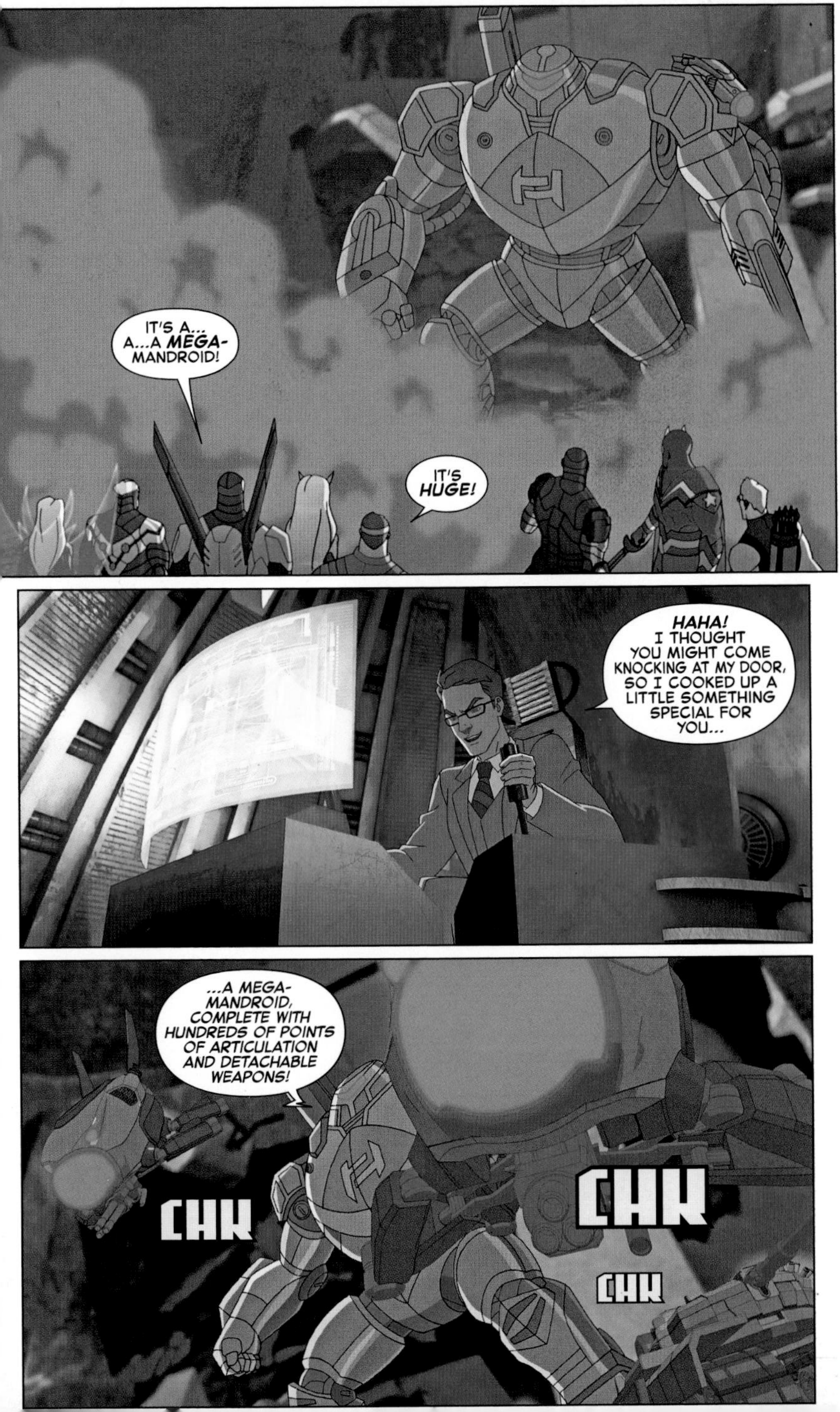
IT'S A... A...A MEGA-MANDROID!
IT'S HUGE!
HAHA! I THOUGHT YOU MIGHT COME KNOCKING AT MY DOOR, SO I COOKED UP A LITTLE SOMETHING SPECIAL FOR YOU...
...A MEGA-MANDROID, COMPLETE WITH HUNDREDS OF POINTS OF ARTICULATION AND DETACHABLE WEAPONS!
CHK
CHK
CHK

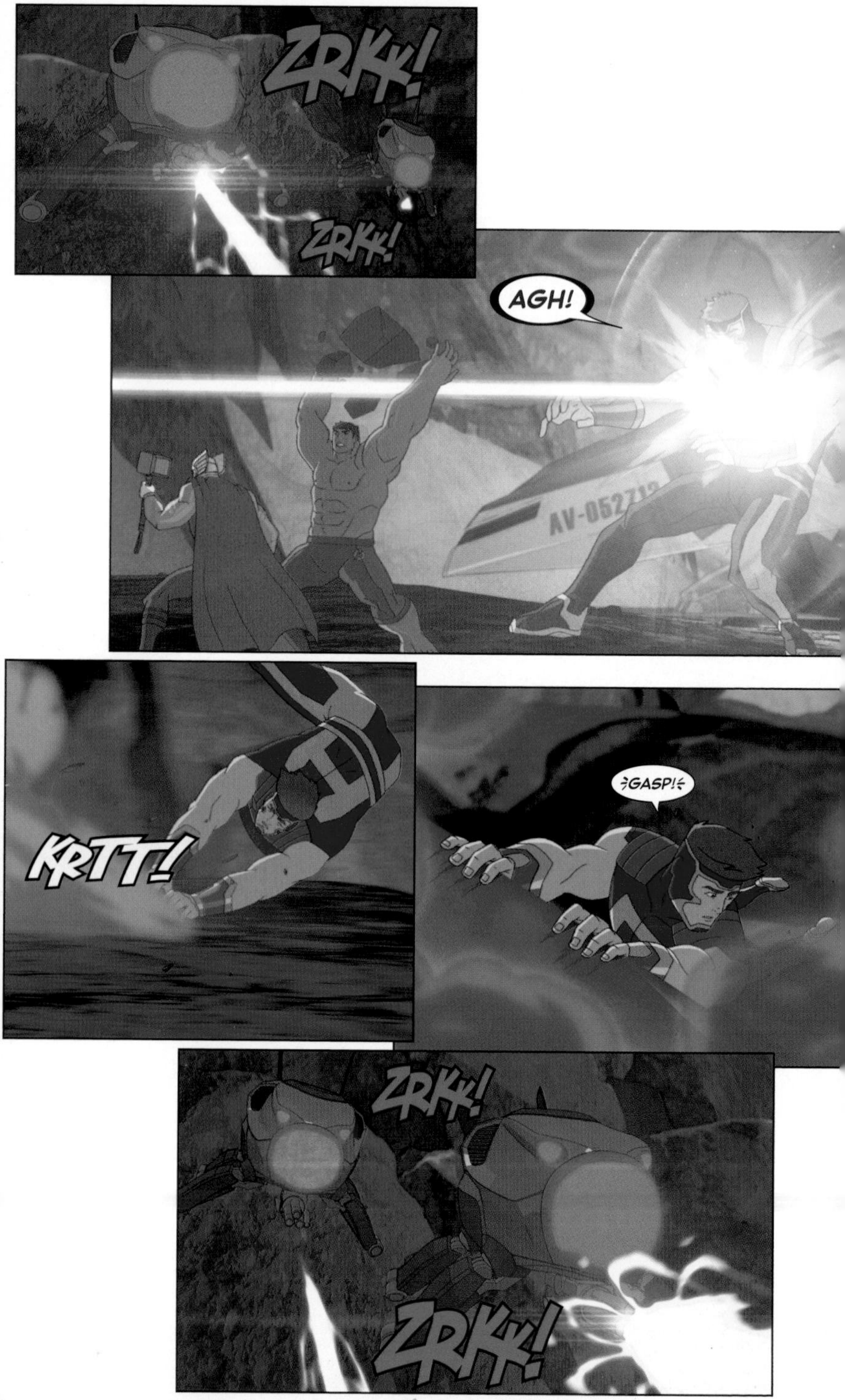
ZRKK!
ZRKK!
AGH!
KRTT!
GASP!
ZRKK!
ZRKK!

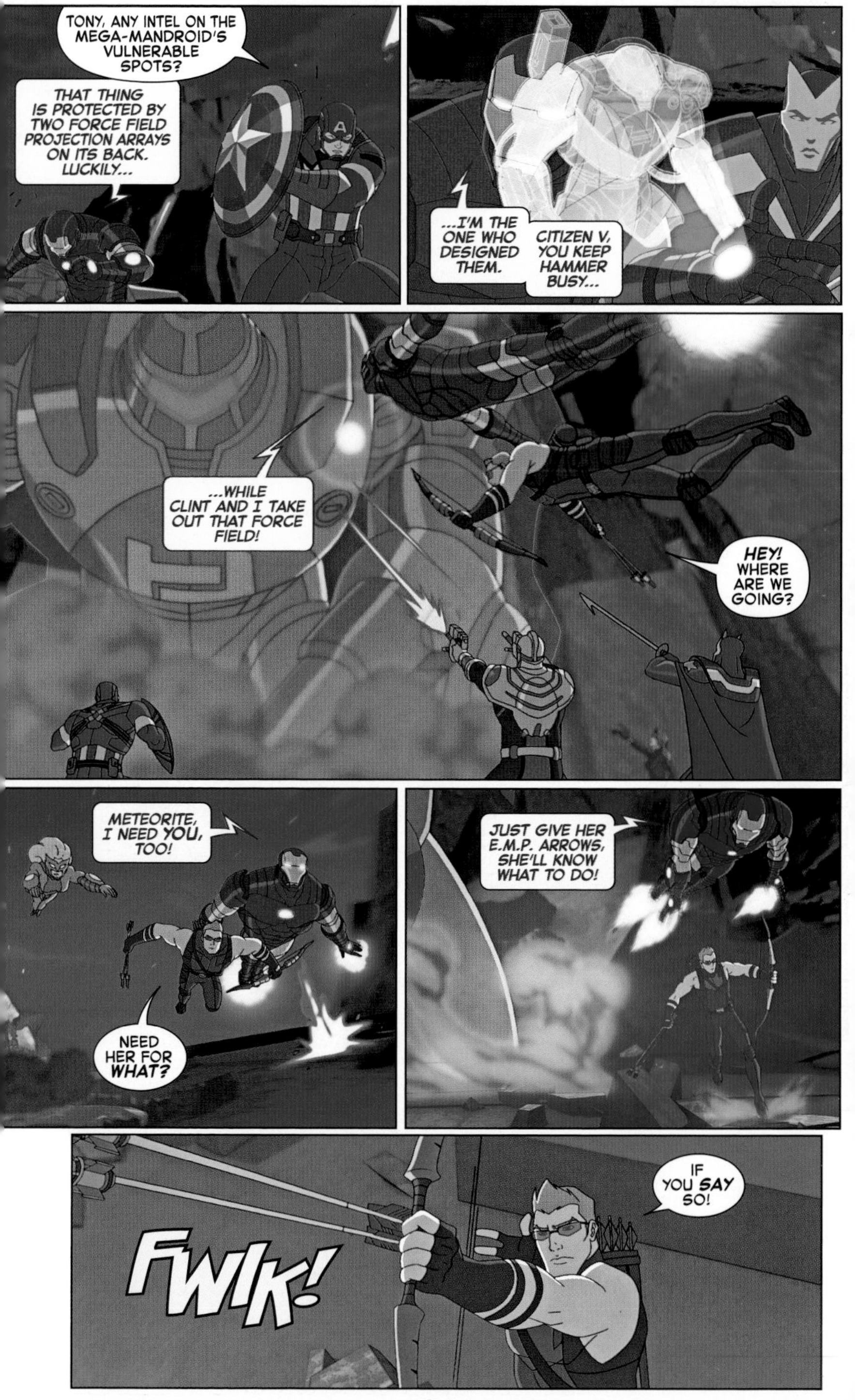

TONY, ANY INTEL ON THE MEGA-MANDROID'S VULNERABLE SPOTS?
THAT THING IS PROTECTED BY TWO FORCE FIELD PROJECTION ARRAYS ON ITS BACK. LUCKILY...
...I'M THE ONE WHO DESIGNED THEM.
CITIZEN V, YOU KEEP HAMMER BUSY...
...WHILE CLINT AND I TAKE OUT THAT FORCE FIELD!
HEY! WHERE ARE WE GOING?
METEORITE, I NEED YOU, TOO!
NEED HER FOR WHAT?
JUST GIVE HER E.M.P. ARROWS, SHE'LL KNOW WHAT TO DO!
IF YOU SAY SO!
FWIK!

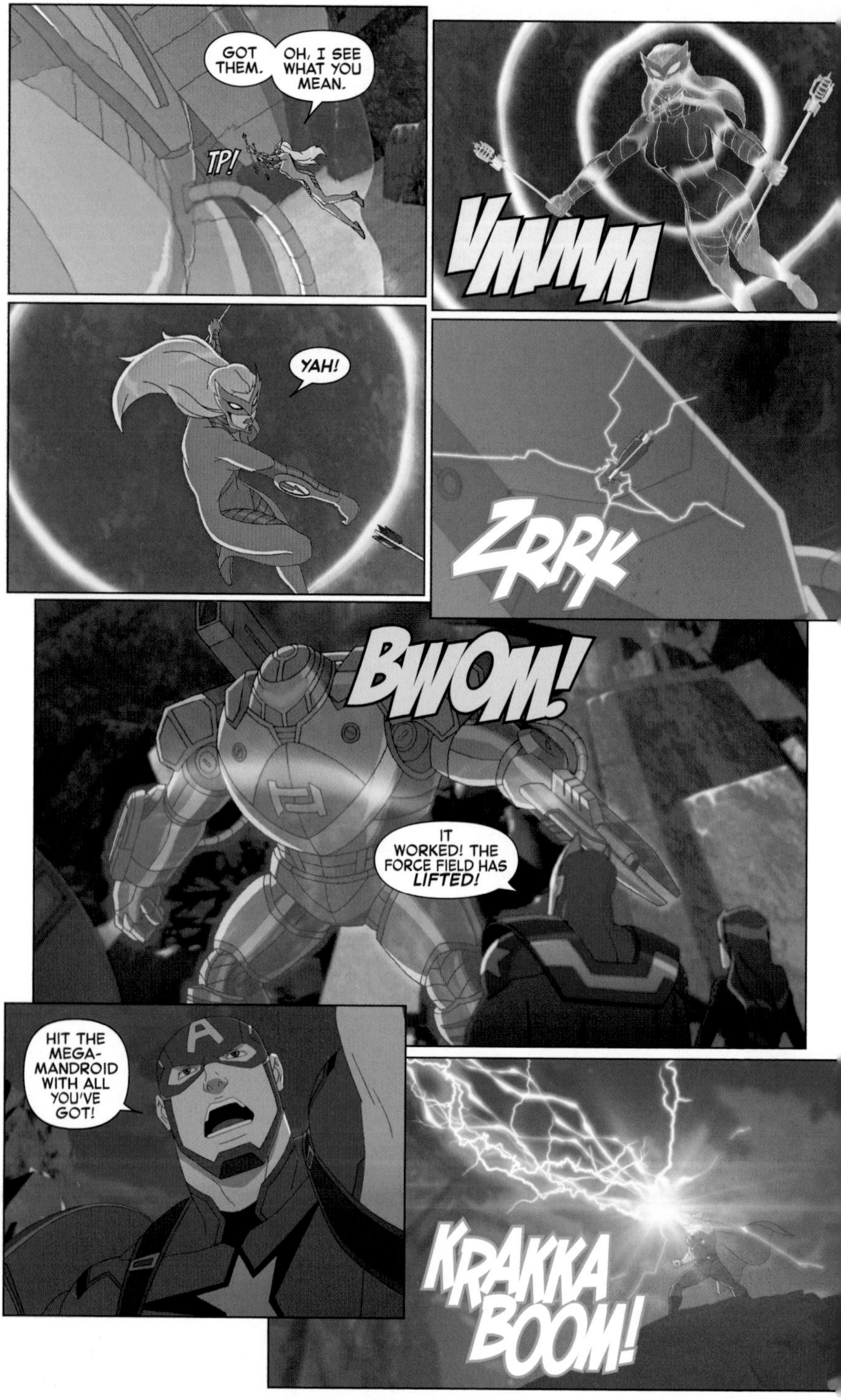
GOT THEM.
OH, I SEE WHAT YOU MEAN.
TP!
VMMMM
YAH!
ZRRK
BWOM!
IT WORKED! THE FORCE FIELD HAS LIFTED!
HIT THE MEGA-MANDROID WITH ALL YOU'VE GOT!
KRAKKA BOOM!

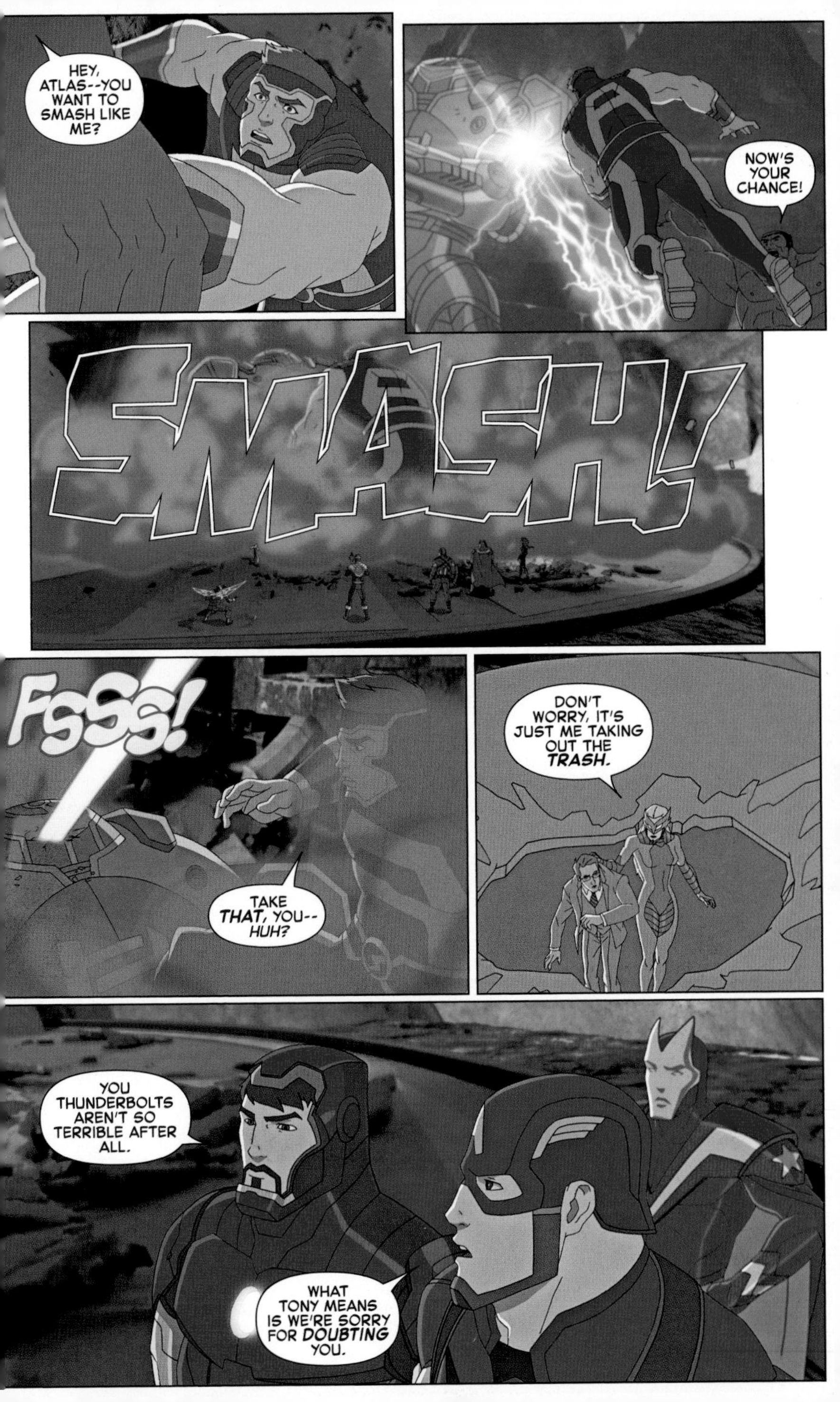
HEY, ATLAS--YOU WANT TO SMASH LIKE ME?
NOW'S YOUR CHANCE!
SMASH!
FSSS!
TAKE THAT, YOU-- HUH?
DON'T WORRY, IT'S JUST ME TAKING OUT THE TRASH.
YOU THUNDERBOLTS AREN'T SO TERRIBLE AFTER ALL.
WHAT TONY MEANS IS WE'RE SORRY FOR DOUBTING YOU.

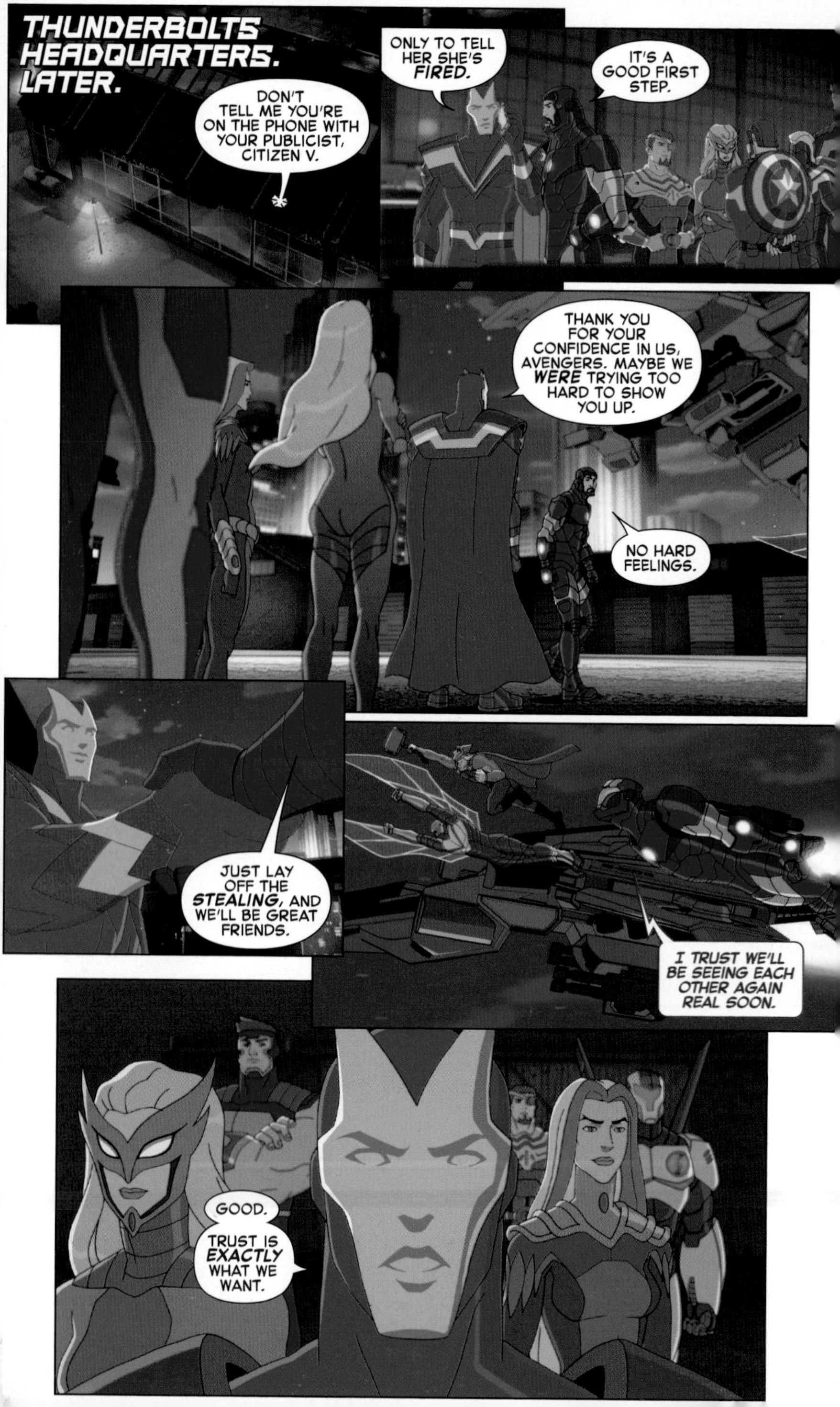
THUNDERBOLTS HEADQUARTERS. LATER.
DON'T TELL ME YOU'RE ON THE PHONE WITH YOUR PUBLICIST, CITIZEN V.
ONLY TO TELL HER SHE'S *FIRED.*
IT'S A GOOD FIRST STEP.
THANK YOU FOR YOUR CONFIDENCE IN US, AVENGERS. MAYBE WE *WERE* TRYING TOO HARD TO SHOW YOU UP.
NO HARD FEELINGS.
JUST LAY OFF THE *STEALING,* AND WE'LL BE GREAT FRIENDS.
I TRUST WE'LL BE SEEING EACH OTHER AGAIN REAL SOON.
GOOD.
TRUST IS *EXACTLY* WHAT WE WANT.

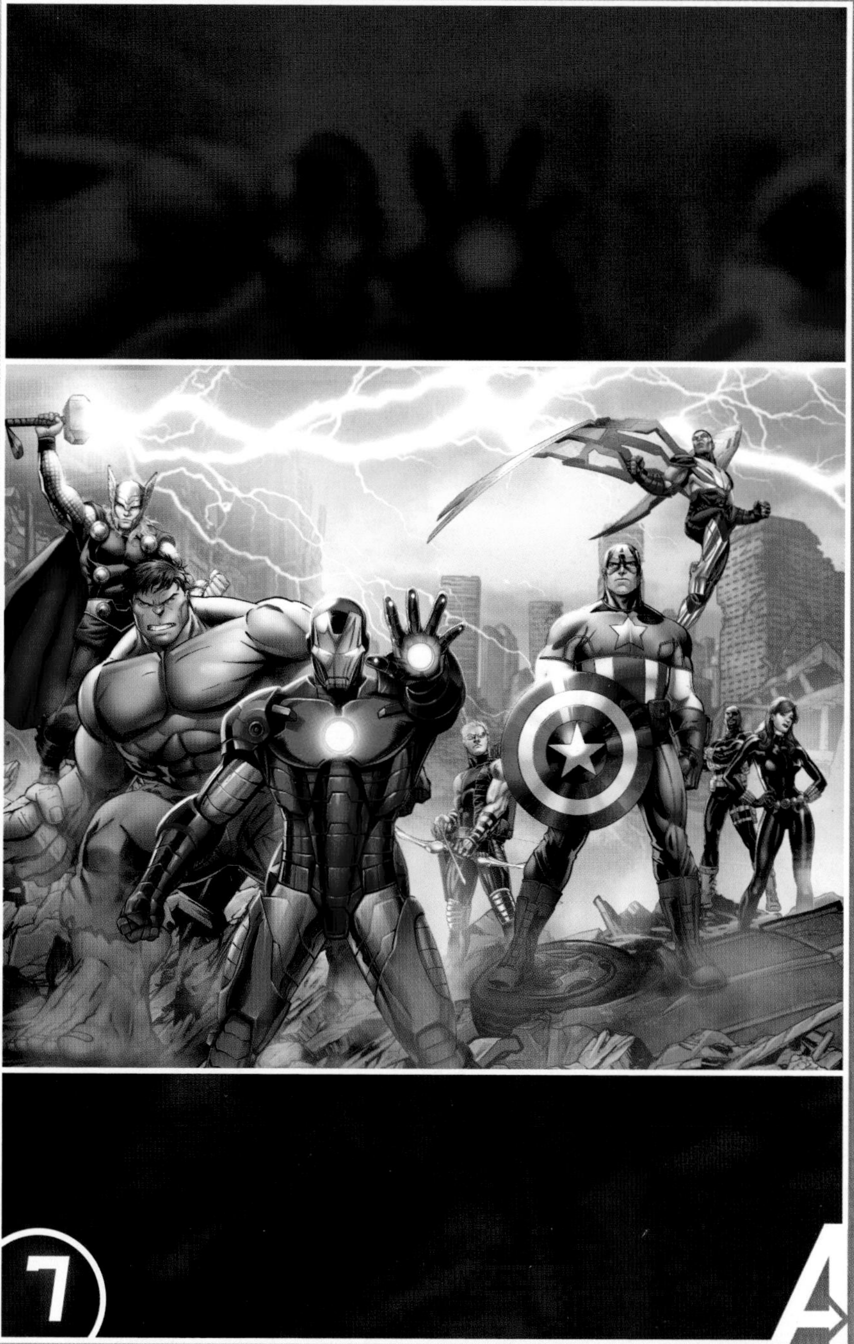
7

THUNDERBOLTS REVEALED

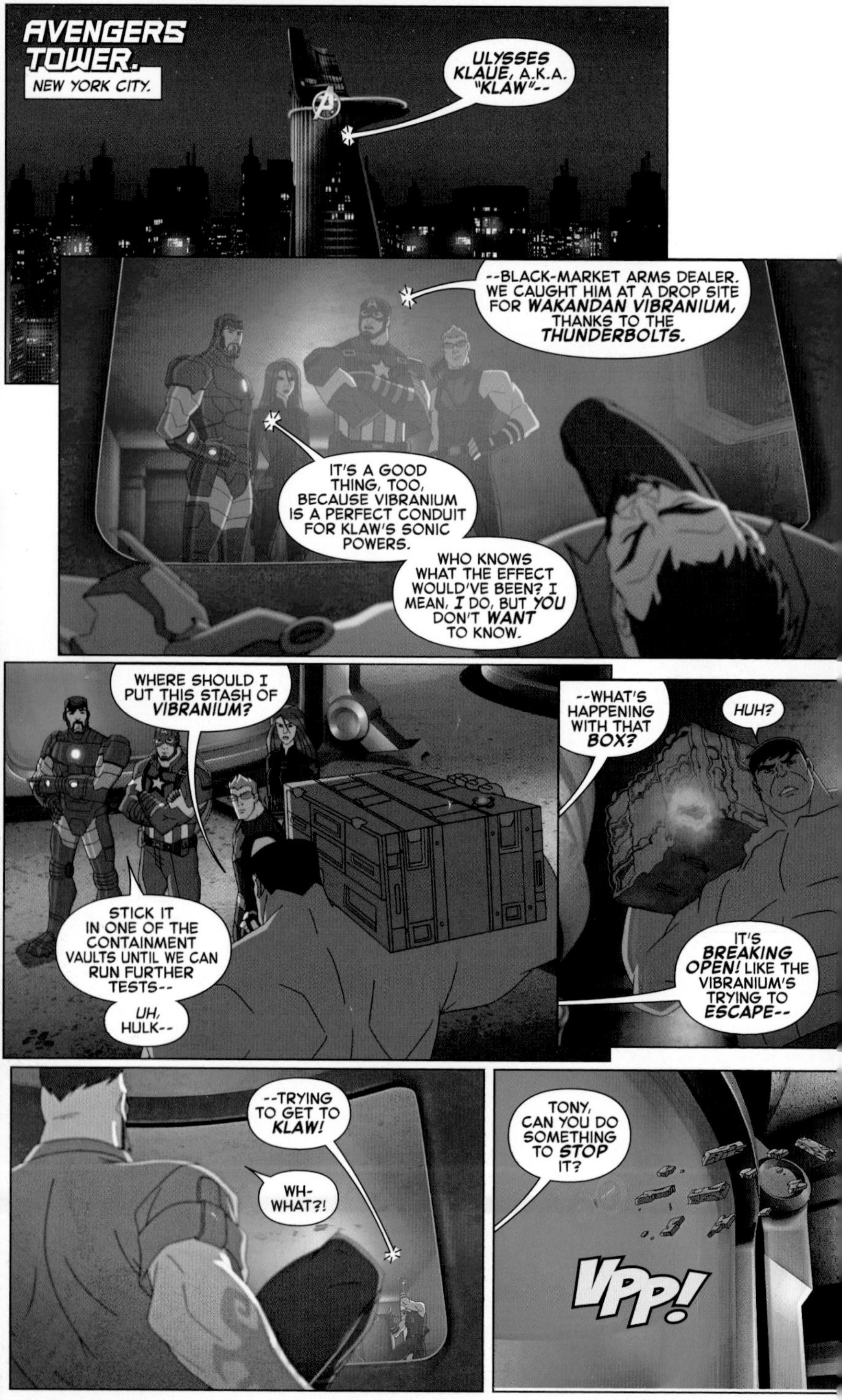
AVENGERS TOWER.
NEW YORK CITY.
ULYSSES KLAUE, A.K.A. "KLAW"--
--BLACK-MARKET ARMS DEALER. WE CAUGHT HIM AT A DROP SITE FOR WAKANDAN VIBRANIUM, THANKS TO THE THUNDERBOLTS.
IT'S A GOOD THING, TOO, BECAUSE VIBRANIUM IS A PERFECT CONDUIT FOR KLAW'S SONIC POWERS.
WHO KNOWS WHAT THE EFFECT WOULD'VE BEEN? I MEAN, I DO, BUT YOU DON'T WANT TO KNOW.
WHERE SHOULD I PUT THIS STASH OF VIBRANIUM?
STICK IT IN ONE OF THE CONTAINMENT VAULTS UNTIL WE CAN RUN FURTHER TESTS--
UH, HULK--
--WHAT'S HAPPENING WITH THAT BOX?
HUH?
IT'S BREAKING OPEN! LIKE THE VIBRANIUM'S TRYING TO ESCAPE--
--TRYING TO GET TO KLAW!
WH- WHAT?!
TONY, CAN YOU DO SOMETHING TO STOP IT?
VPP!

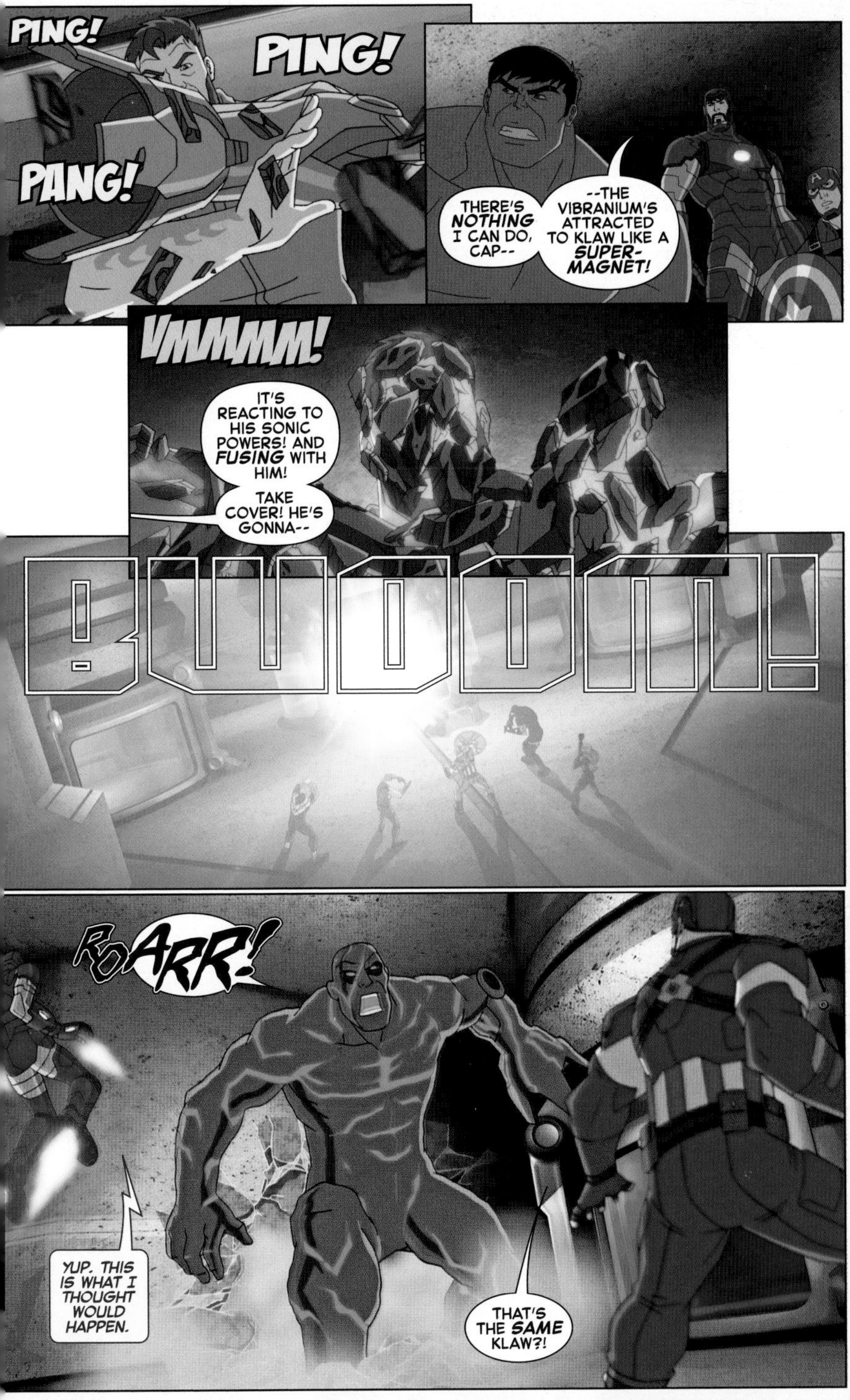
PING!
PING!
PANG!
THERE'S NOTHING I CAN DO, CAP--
--THE VIBRANIUM'S ATTRACTED TO KLAW LIKE A SUPER-MAGNET!
VMMMM!
IT'S REACTING TO HIS SONIC POWERS! AND FUSING WITH HIM!
TAKE COVER! HE'S GONNA--
BWOOM!
ROARR!
YUP. THIS IS WHAT I THOUGHT WOULD HAPPEN.
THAT'S THE SAME KLAW?!

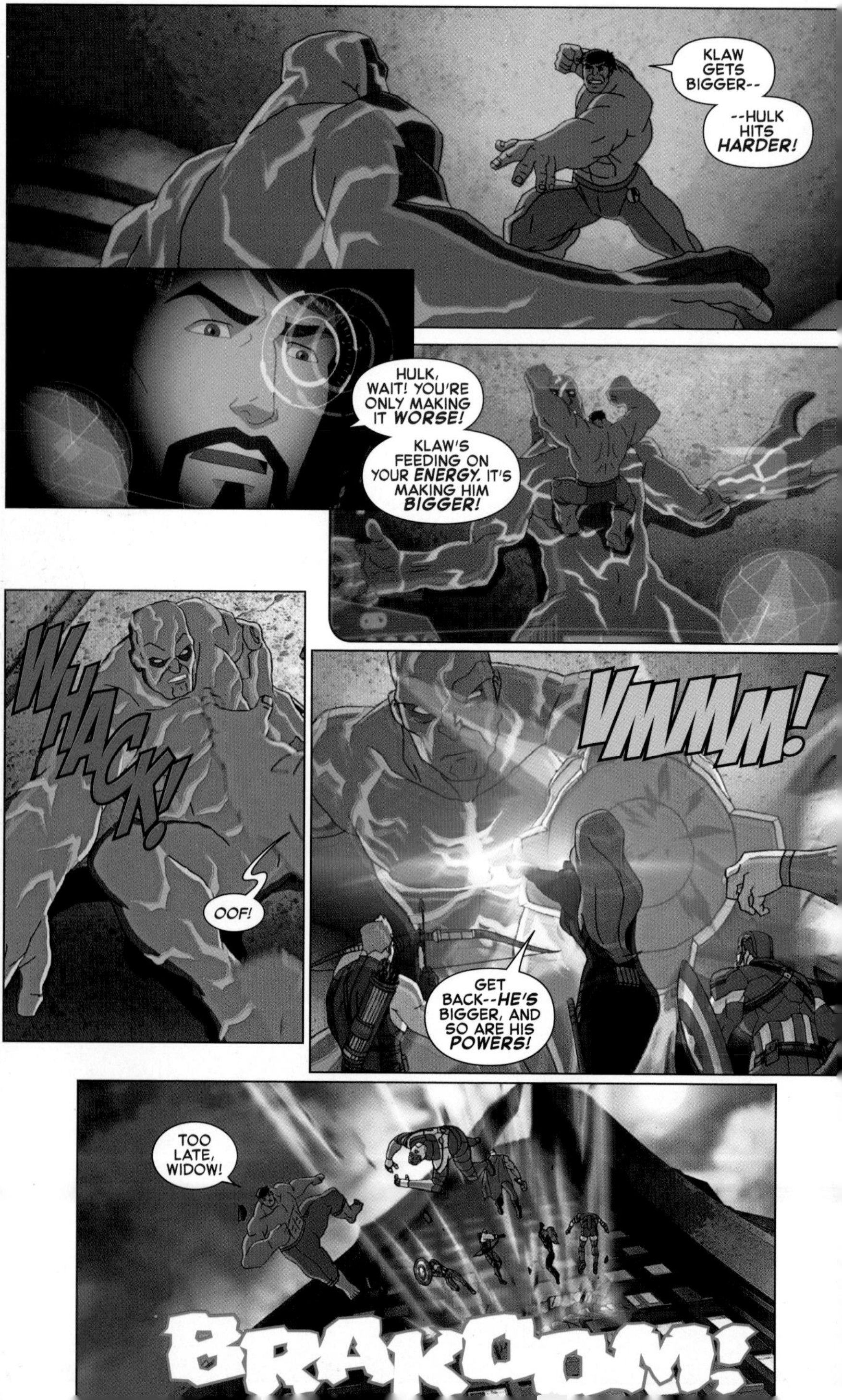
KLAW GETS BIGGER--
--HULK HITS HARDER!
HULK, WAIT! YOU'RE ONLY MAKING IT WORSE!
KLAW'S FEEDING ON YOUR ENERGY. IT'S MAKING HIM BIGGER!
WHACK!
OOF!
VMMM!
GET BACK--HE'S BIGGER, AND SO ARE HIS POWERS!
TOO LATE, WIDOW!
BRAKOOM!

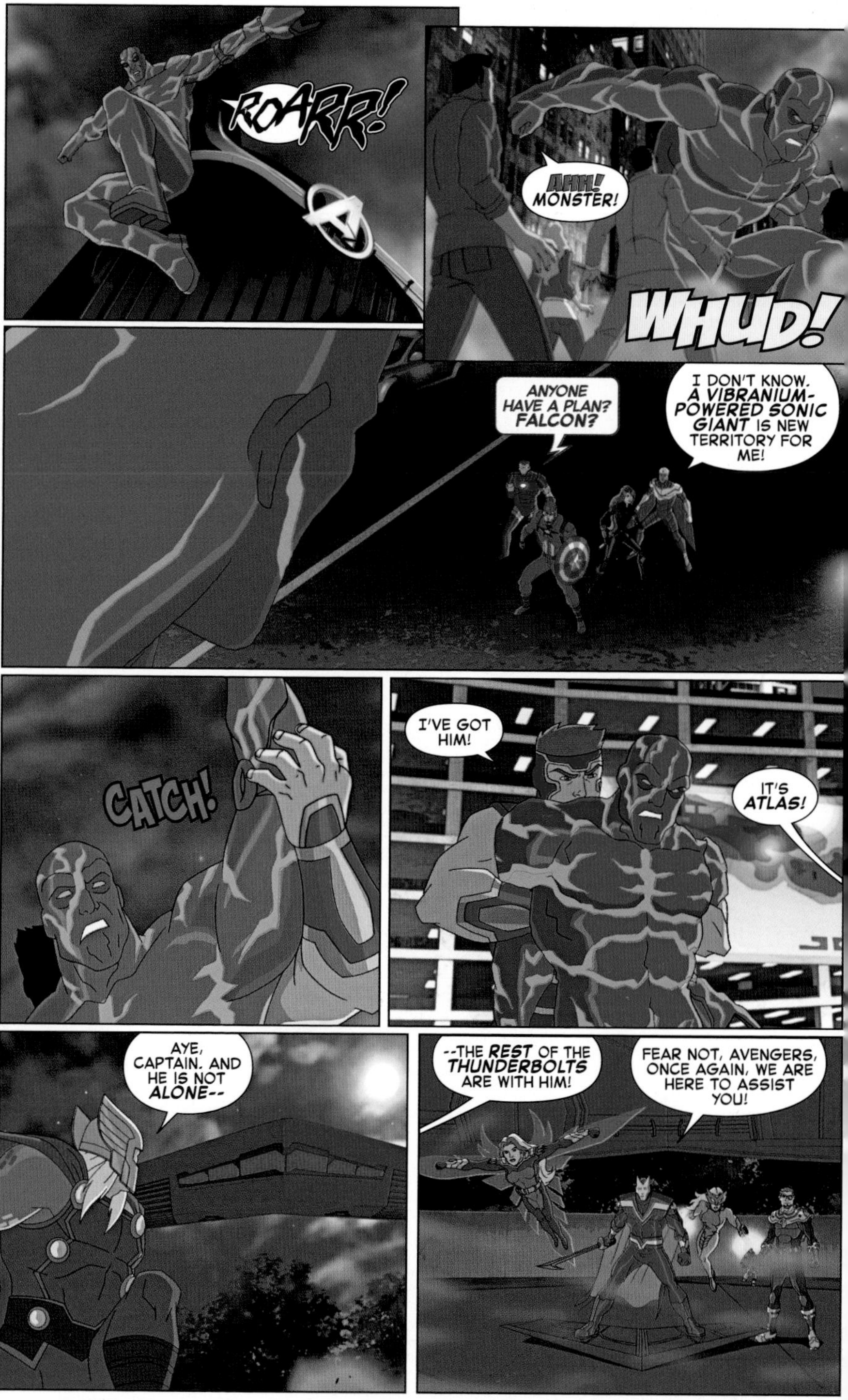
ROARR!
AHH! MONSTER!
WHUD!
ANYONE HAVE A PLAN? FALCON?
I DON'T KNOW. A VIBRANIUM-POWERED SONIC GIANT IS NEW TERRITORY FOR ME!
CATCH!
I'VE GOT HIM!
IT'S ATLAS!
AYE, CAPTAIN. AND HE IS NOT ALONE--
--THE REST OF THE THUNDERBOLTS ARE WITH HIM!
FEAR NOT, AVENGERS, ONCE AGAIN, WE ARE HERE TO ASSIST YOU!

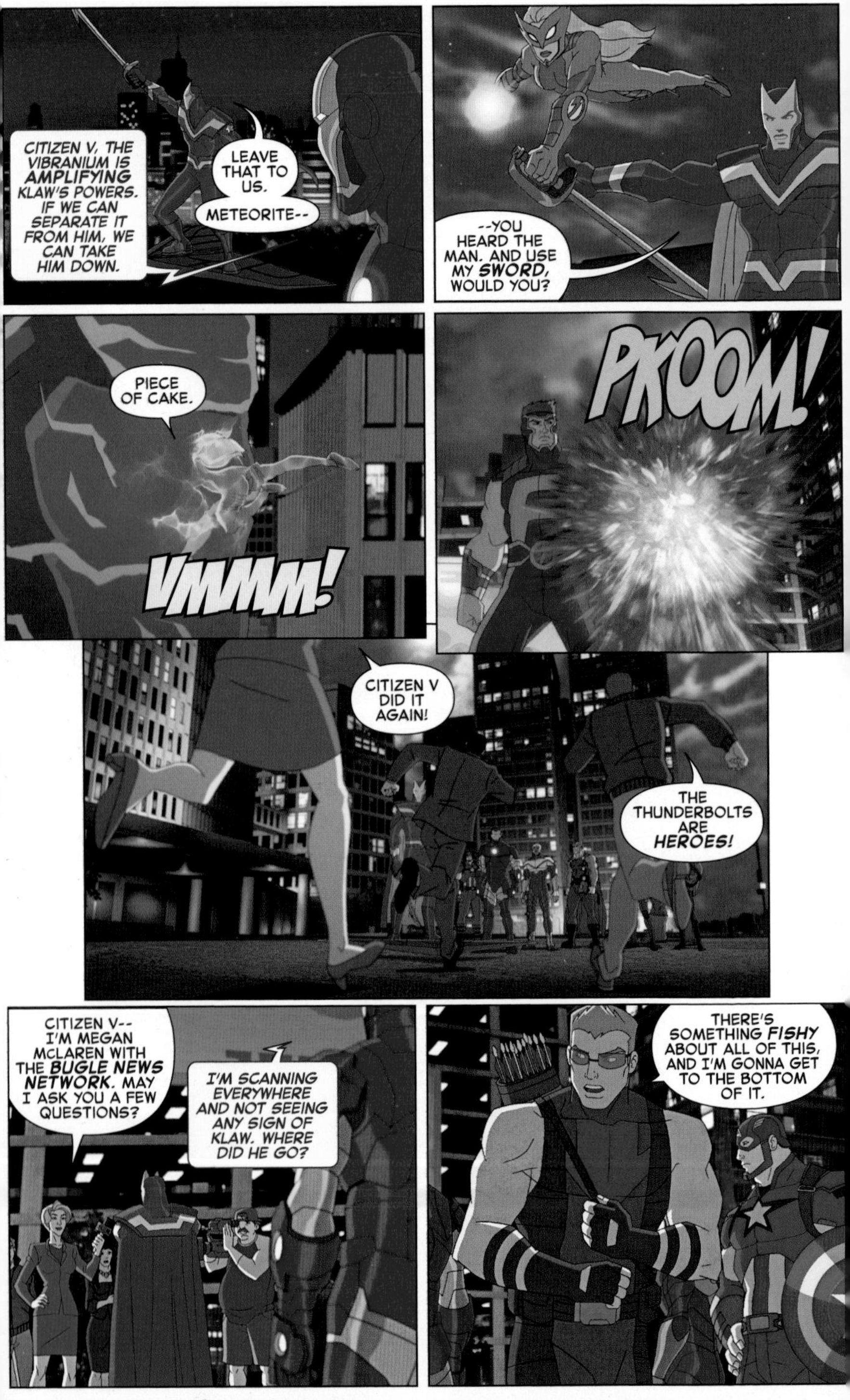

CITIZEN V, THE VIBRANIUM IS AMPLIFYING KLAW'S POWERS. IF WE CAN SEPARATE IT FROM HIM, WE CAN TAKE HIM DOWN.
LEAVE THAT TO US.
METEORITE--
--YOU HEARD THE MAN. AND USE MY SWORD, WOULD YOU?
PIECE OF CAKE.
VMMM!
PKOOM!
CITIZEN V DID IT AGAIN!
THE THUNDERBOLTS ARE HEROES!
CITIZEN V-- I'M MEGAN McLAREN WITH THE BUGLE NEWS NETWORK. MAY I ASK YOU A FEW QUESTIONS?
I'M SCANNING EVERYWHERE AND NOT SEEING ANY SIGN OF KLAW. WHERE DID HE GO?
THERE'S SOMETHING FISHY ABOUT ALL OF THIS, AND I'M GONNA GET TO THE BOTTOM OF IT.

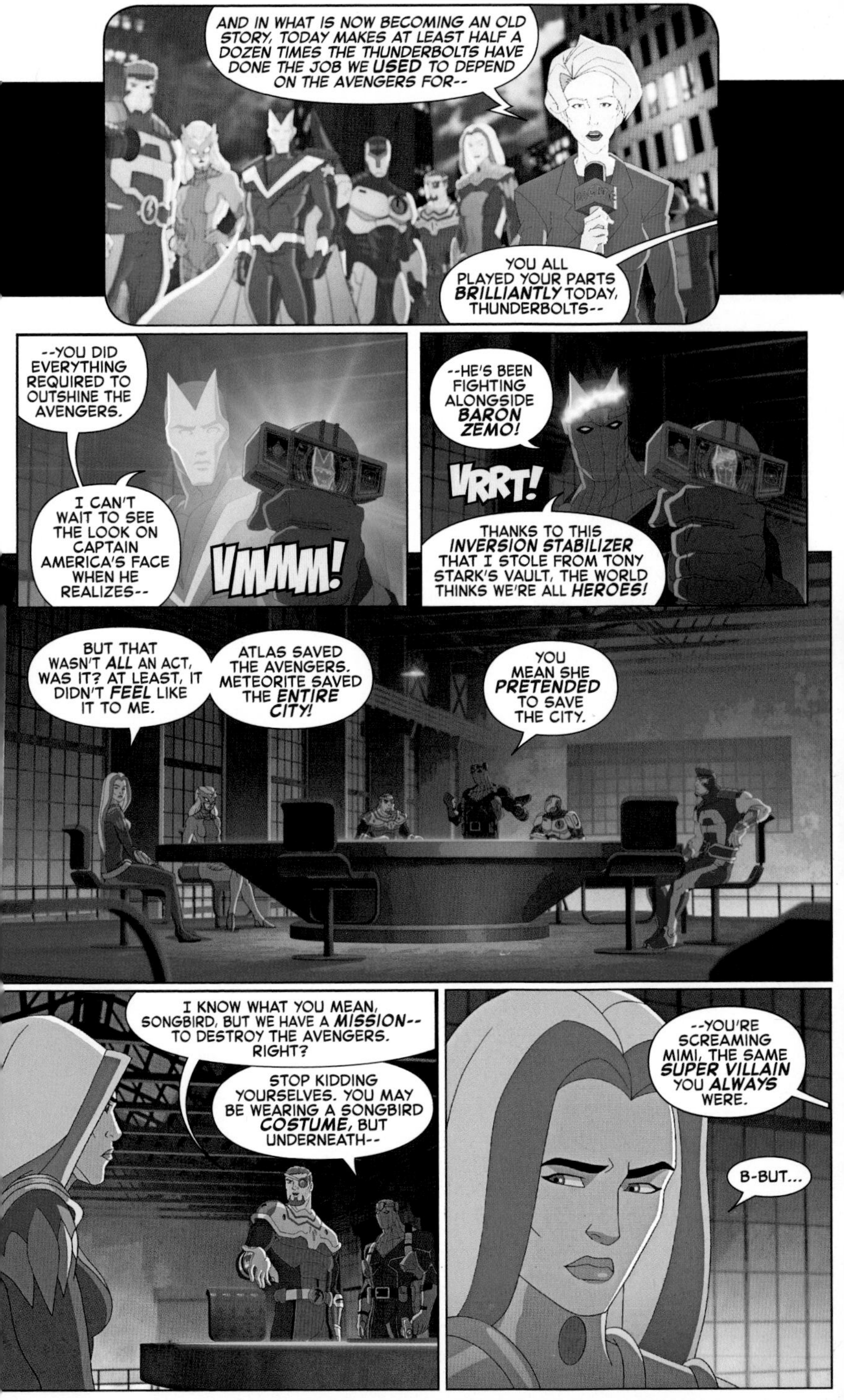
AND IN WHAT IS NOW BECOMING AN OLD STORY, TODAY MAKES AT LEAST HALF A DOZEN TIMES THE THUNDERBOLTS HAVE DONE THE JOB WE USED TO DEPEND ON THE AVENGERS FOR--
YOU ALL PLAYED YOUR PARTS BRILLIANTLY TODAY, THUNDERBOLTS--
--YOU DID EVERYTHING REQUIRED TO OUTSHINE THE AVENGERS.
I CAN'T WAIT TO SEE THE LOOK ON CAPTAIN AMERICA'S FACE WHEN HE REALIZES--
VMMM!
--HE'S BEEN FIGHTING ALONGSIDE BARON ZEMO!
VRRT!
THANKS TO THIS INVERSION STABILIZER THAT I STOLE FROM TONY STARK'S VAULT, THE WORLD THINKS WE'RE ALL HEROES!
BUT THAT WASN'T ALL AN ACT, WAS IT? AT LEAST, IT DIDN'T FEEL LIKE IT TO ME.
ATLAS SAVED THE AVENGERS. METEORITE SAVED THE ENTIRE CITY!
YOU MEAN SHE PRETENDED TO SAVE THE CITY.
I KNOW WHAT YOU MEAN, SONGBIRD, BUT WE HAVE A MISSION-- TO DESTROY THE AVENGERS. RIGHT?
STOP KIDDING YOURSELVES. YOU MAY BE WEARING A SONGBIRD COSTUME, BUT UNDERNEATH--
--YOU'RE SCREAMING MIMI, THE SAME SUPER VILLAIN YOU ALWAYS WERE.
B-BUT...

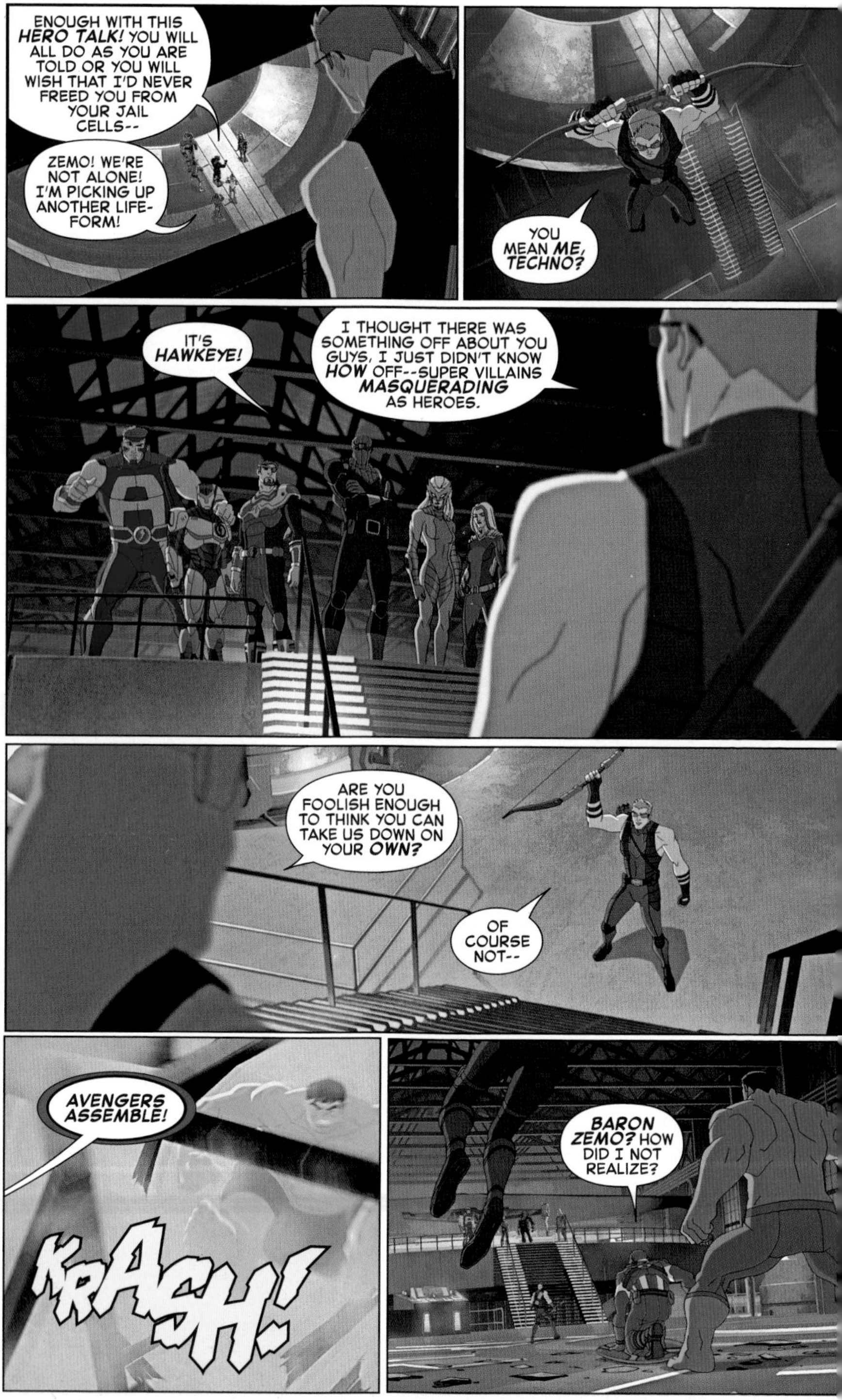

ENOUGH WITH THIS HERO TALK! YOU WILL ALL DO AS YOU ARE TOLD OR YOU WILL WISH THAT I'D NEVER FREED YOU FROM YOUR JAIL CELLS--
ZEMO! WE'RE NOT ALONE! I'M PICKING UP ANOTHER LIFE-FORM!
YOU MEAN ME, TECHNO?
IT'S HAWKEYE!
I THOUGHT THERE WAS SOMETHING OFF ABOUT YOU GUYS, I JUST DIDN'T KNOW HOW OFF--SUPER VILLAINS MASQUERADING AS HEROES.
ARE YOU FOOLISH ENOUGH TO THINK YOU CAN TAKE US DOWN ON YOUR OWN?
OF COURSE NOT--
AVENGERS ASSEMBLE!
KRASH!
BARON ZEMO? HOW DID I NOT REALIZE?

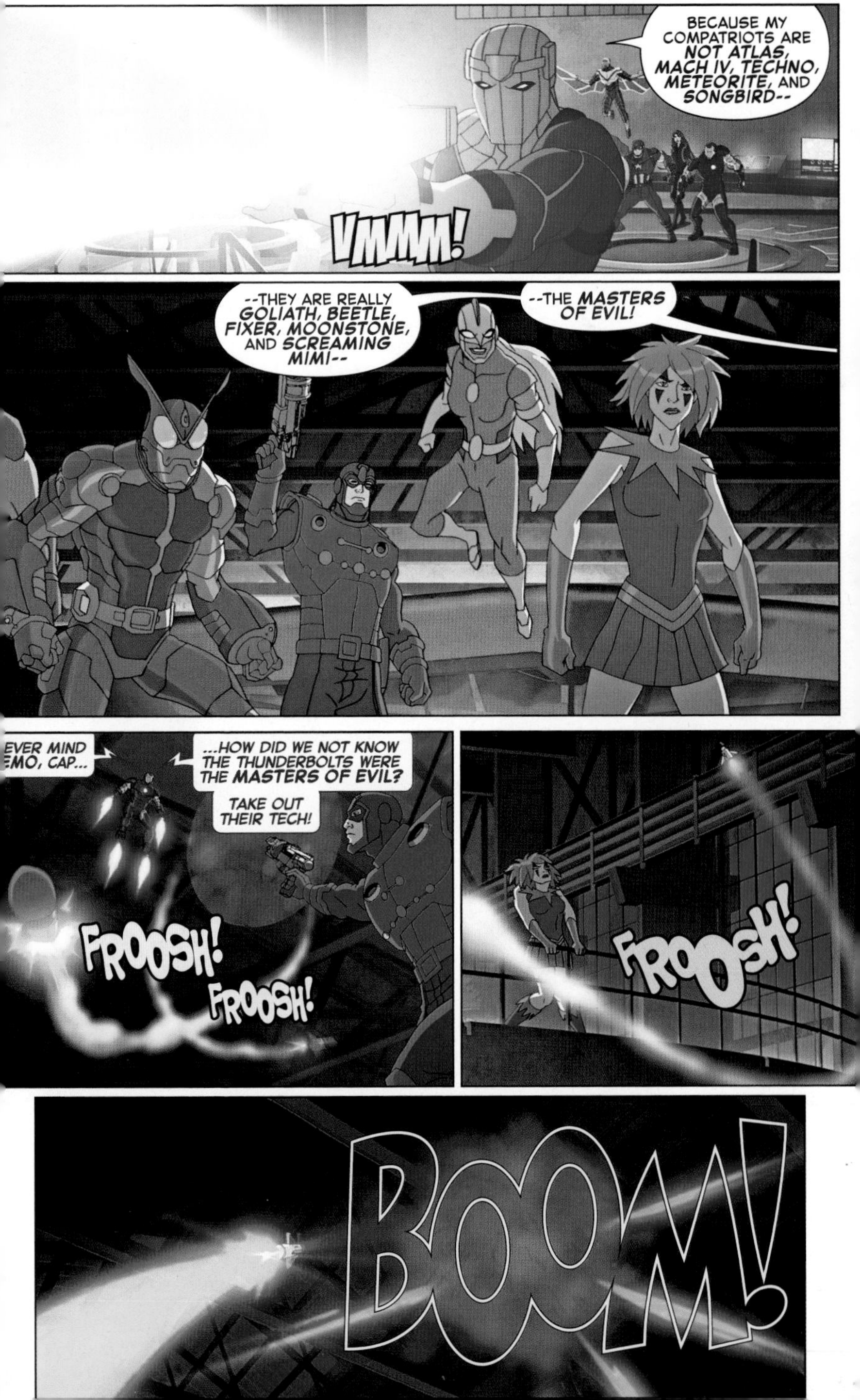
BECAUSE MY COMPATRIOTS ARE NOT ATLAS, MACH IV, TECHNO, METEORITE, AND SONGBIRD--
VMMM!
--THEY ARE REALLY GOLIATH, BEETLE, FIXER, MOONSTONE, AND SCREAMING MIMI--
--THE MASTERS OF EVIL!
EVER MIND
EMO, CAP...
...HOW DID WE NOT KNOW THE THUNDERBOLTS WERE THE MASTERS OF EVIL?
TAKE OUT THEIR TECH!
FROOSH!
FROOSH!
FROOSH!
BOOM!

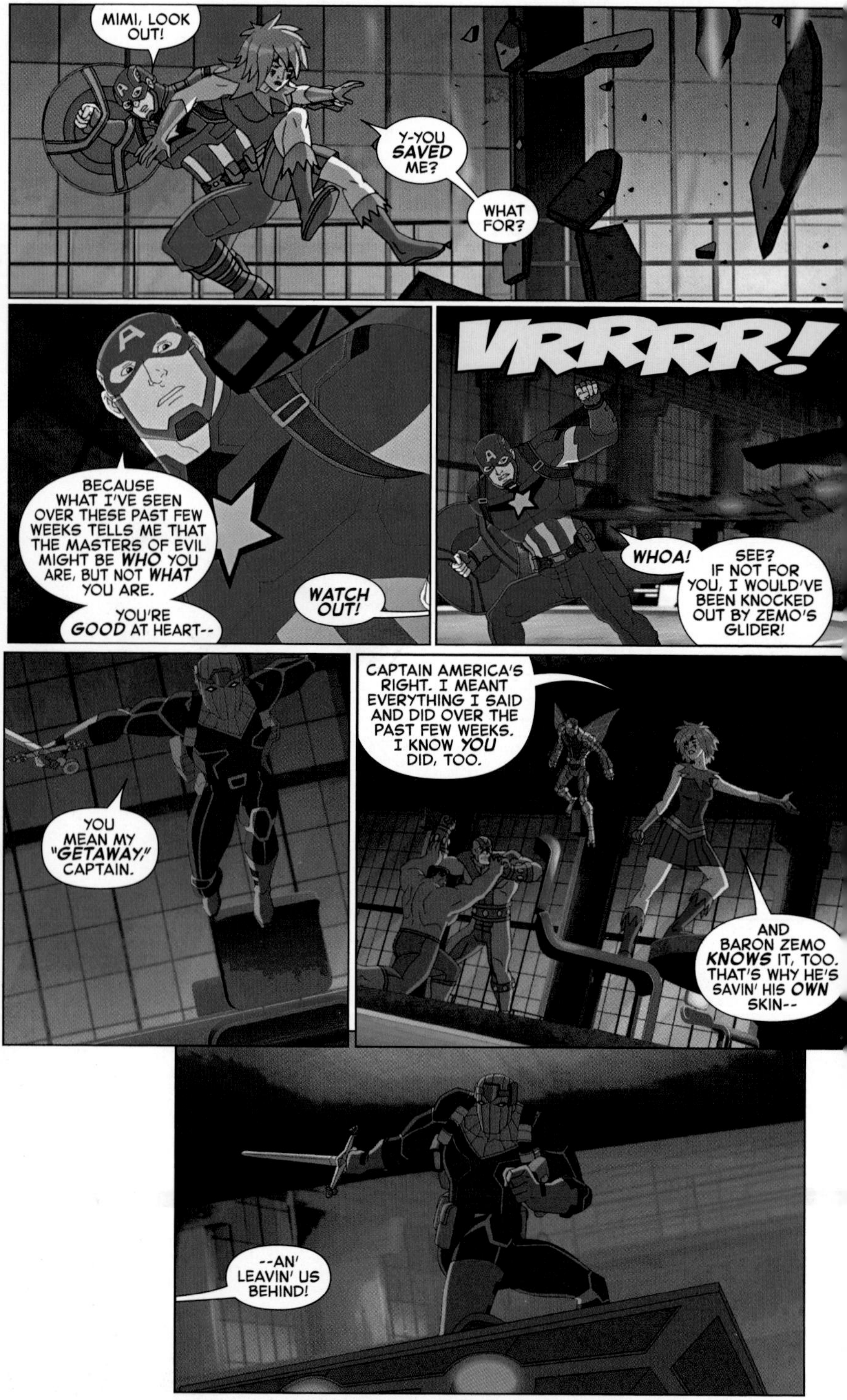
MIMI, LOOK OUT!
Y-YOU SAVED ME?
WHAT FOR?
BECAUSE WHAT I'VE SEEN OVER THESE PAST FEW WEEKS TELLS ME THAT THE MASTERS OF EVIL MIGHT BE WHO YOU ARE, BUT NOT WHAT YOU ARE.
YOU'RE GOOD AT HEART--
WATCH OUT!
VRRRR!
WHOA!
SEE? IF NOT FOR YOU, I WOULD'VE BEEN KNOCKED OUT BY ZEMO'S GLIDER!
YOU MEAN MY "GETAWAY," CAPTAIN.
CAPTAIN AMERICA'S RIGHT. I MEANT EVERYTHING I SAID AND DID OVER THE PAST FEW WEEKS. I KNOW YOU DID, TOO.
AND BARON ZEMO KNOWS IT, TOO. THAT'S WHY HE'S SAVIN' HIS OWN SKIN--
--AN' LEAVIN' US BEHIND!

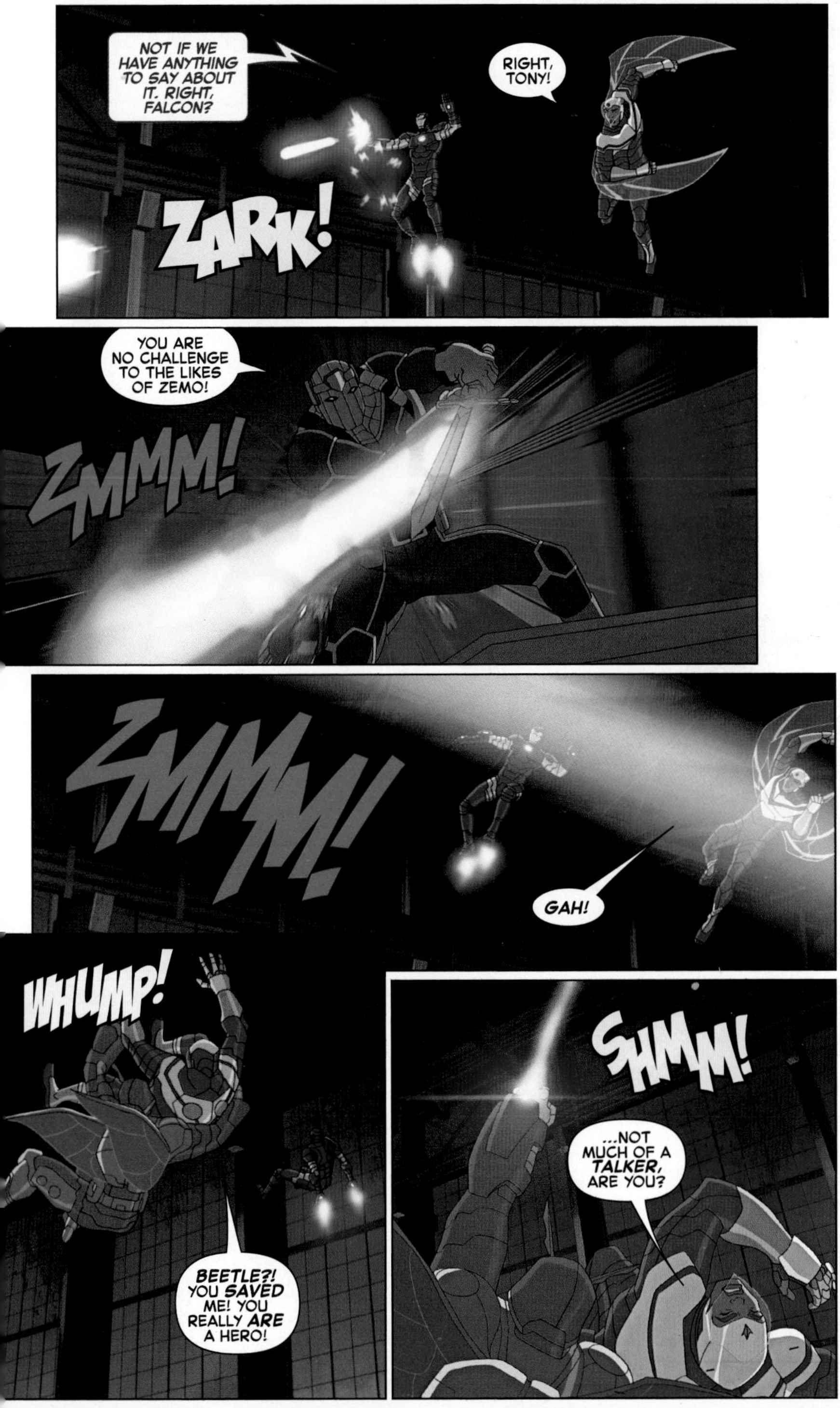
NOT IF WE HAVE ANYTHING TO SAY ABOUT IT. RIGHT, FALCON?
RIGHT, TONY!
ZARK!
YOU ARE NO CHALLENGE TO THE LIKES OF ZEMO!
ZMMM!
ZMMM!
GAH!
WHUMP!
BEETLE?! YOU SAVED ME! YOU REALLY ARE A HERO!
SHMM!
...NOT MUCH OF A TALKER, ARE YOU?

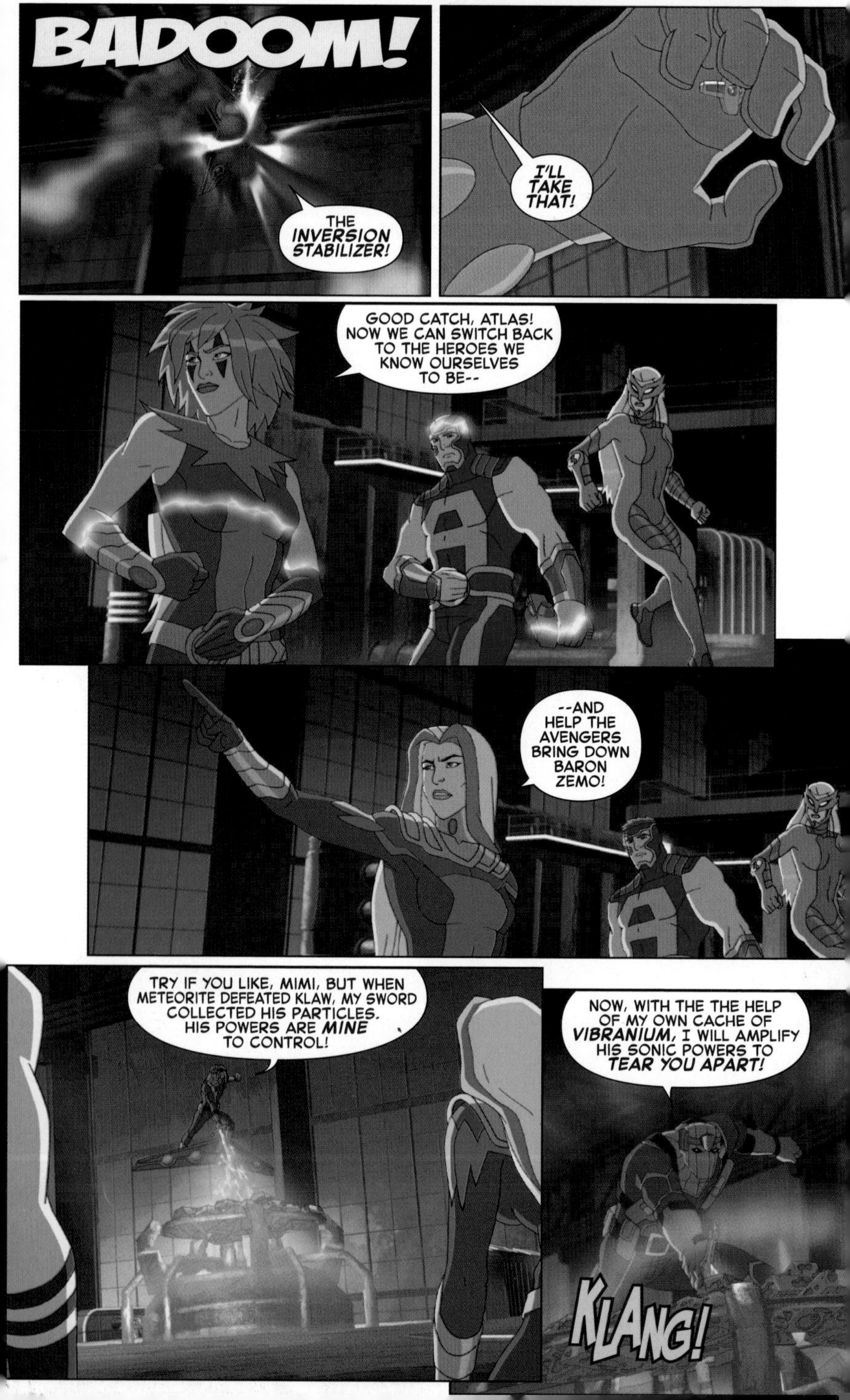
BADOOM!
THE INVERSION STABILIZER!
I'LL TAKE THAT!
GOOD CATCH, ATLAS! NOW WE CAN SWITCH BACK TO THE HEROES WE KNOW OURSELVES TO BE--
--AND HELP THE AVENGERS BRING DOWN BARON ZEMO!
TRY IF YOU LIKE, MIMI, BUT WHEN METEORITE DEFEATED KLAW, MY SWORD COLLECTED HIS PARTICLES. HIS POWERS ARE MINE TO CONTROL!
NOW, WITH THE THE HELP OF MY OWN CACHE OF VIBRANIUM, I WILL AMPLIFY HIS SONIC POWERS TO TEAR YOU APART!
KLANG!

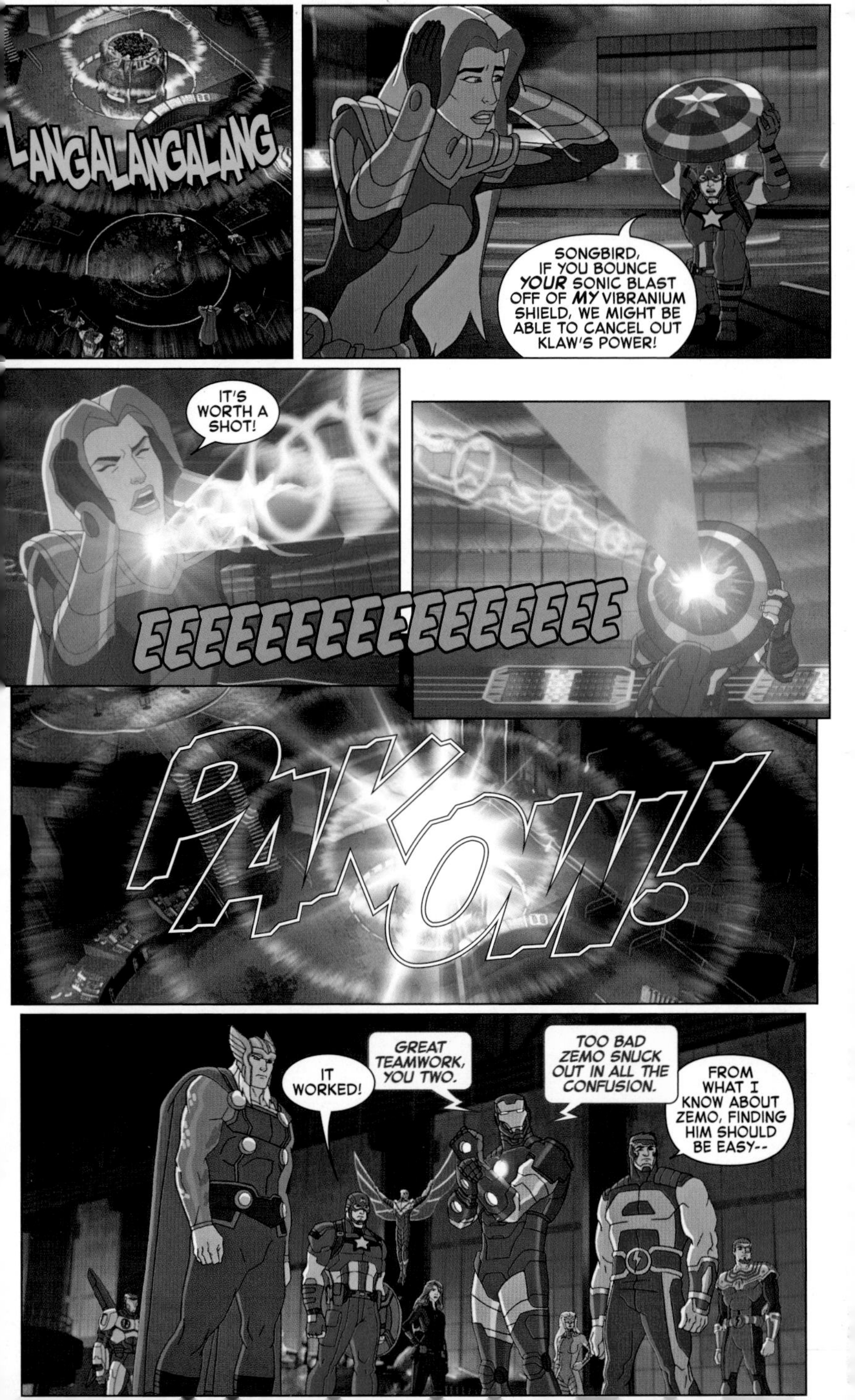

LANGALANGALANG
SONGBIRD, IF YOU BOUNCE YOUR SONIC BLAST OFF OF MY VIBRANIUM SHIELD, WE MIGHT BE ABLE TO CANCEL OUT KLAW'S POWER!
IT'S WORTH A SHOT!
EEEEEEEEEEEEEEEE
PAKOWW!
IT WORKED!
GREAT TEAMWORK, YOU TWO.
TOO BAD ZEMO SNUCK OUT IN ALL THE CONFUSION.
FROM WHAT I KNOW ABOUT ZEMO, FINDING HIM SHOULD BE EASY--

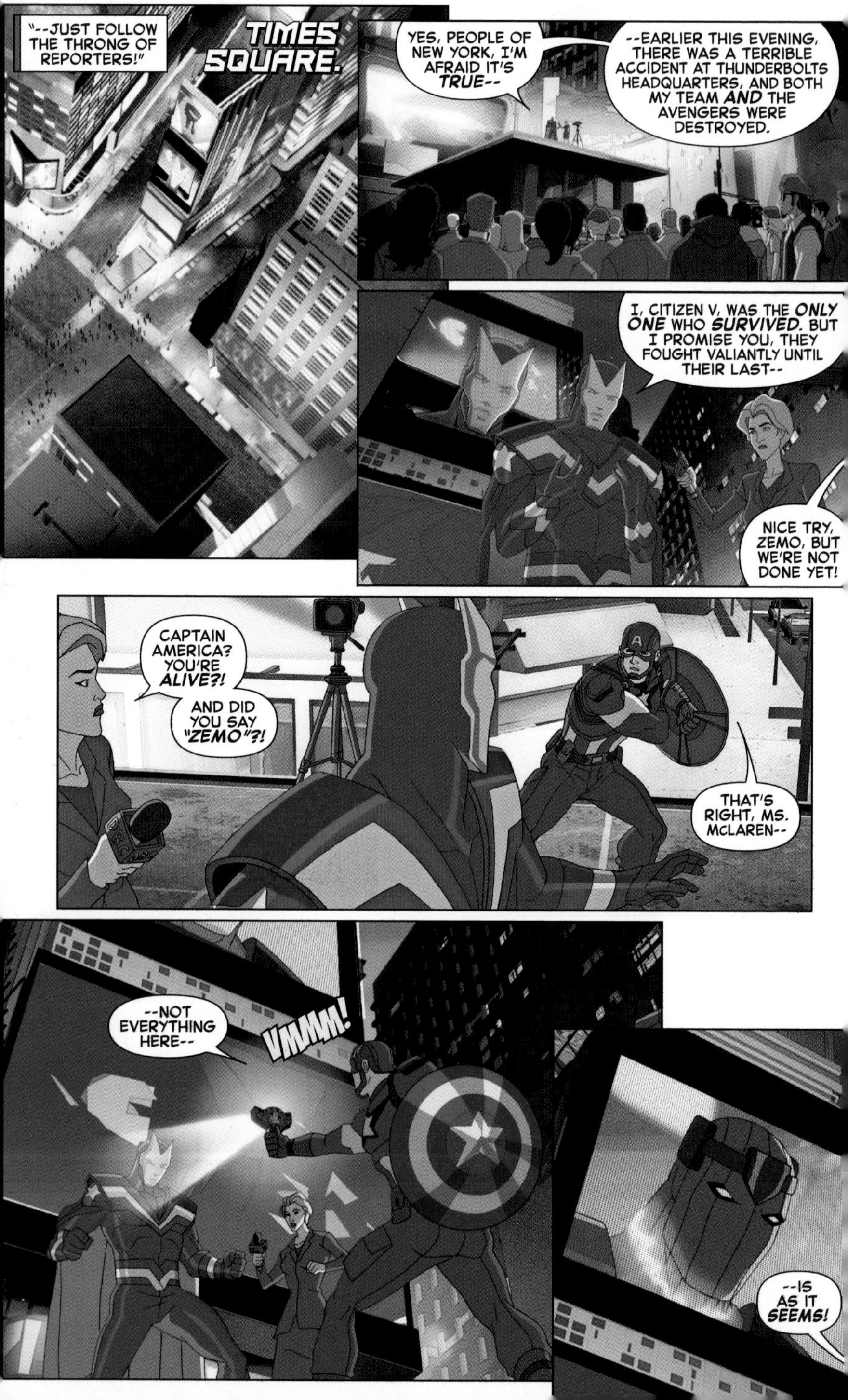
"--JUST FOLLOW THE THRONG OF REPORTERS!"
TIMES SQUARE.
YES, PEOPLE OF NEW YORK, I'M AFRAID IT'S TRUE--
--EARLIER THIS EVENING, THERE WAS A TERRIBLE ACCIDENT AT THUNDERBOLTS HEADQUARTERS, AND BOTH MY TEAM AND THE AVENGERS WERE DESTROYED.
I, CITIZEN V, WAS THE ONLY ONE WHO SURVIVED. BUT I PROMISE YOU, THEY FOUGHT VALIANTLY UNTIL THEIR LAST--
NICE TRY, ZEMO, BUT WE'RE NOT DONE YET!
CAPTAIN AMERICA? YOU'RE ALIVE?!
AND DID YOU SAY "ZEMO"?!
THAT'S RIGHT, MS. MCLAREN--
--NOT EVERYTHING HERE--
VMMM!
--IS AS IT SEEMS!

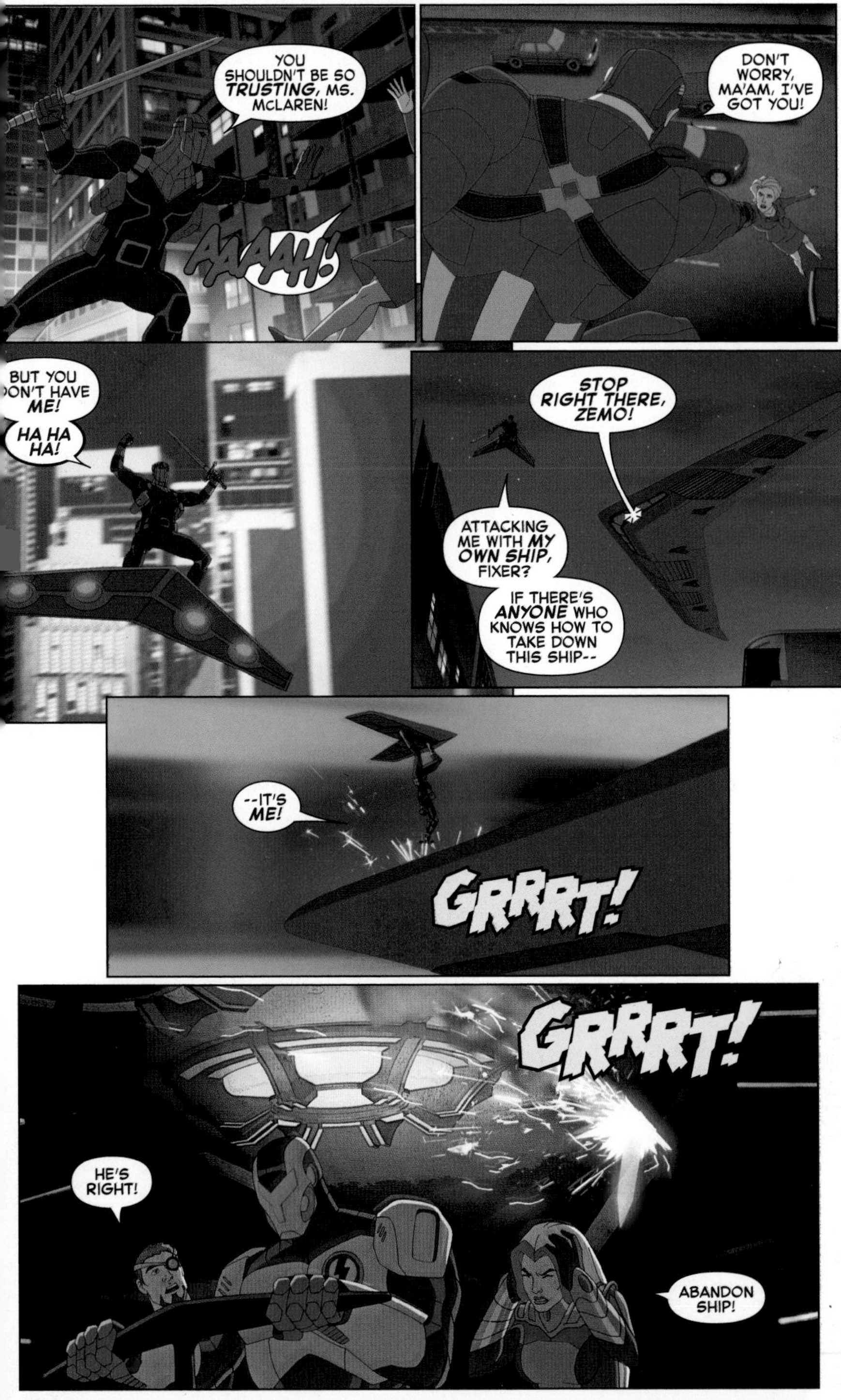
YOU SHOULDN'T BE SO TRUSTING, MS. McLAREN!
AAAAH!
DON'T WORRY, MA'AM, I'VE GOT YOU!
BUT YOU DON'T HAVE ME!
HA HA HA!
STOP RIGHT THERE, ZEMO!
ATTACKING ME WITH MY OWN SHIP, FIXER?
IF THERE'S ANYONE WHO KNOWS HOW TO TAKE DOWN THIS SHIP--
--IT'S ME!
GRRRT!
GRRRT!
HE'S RIGHT!
ABANDON SHIP!

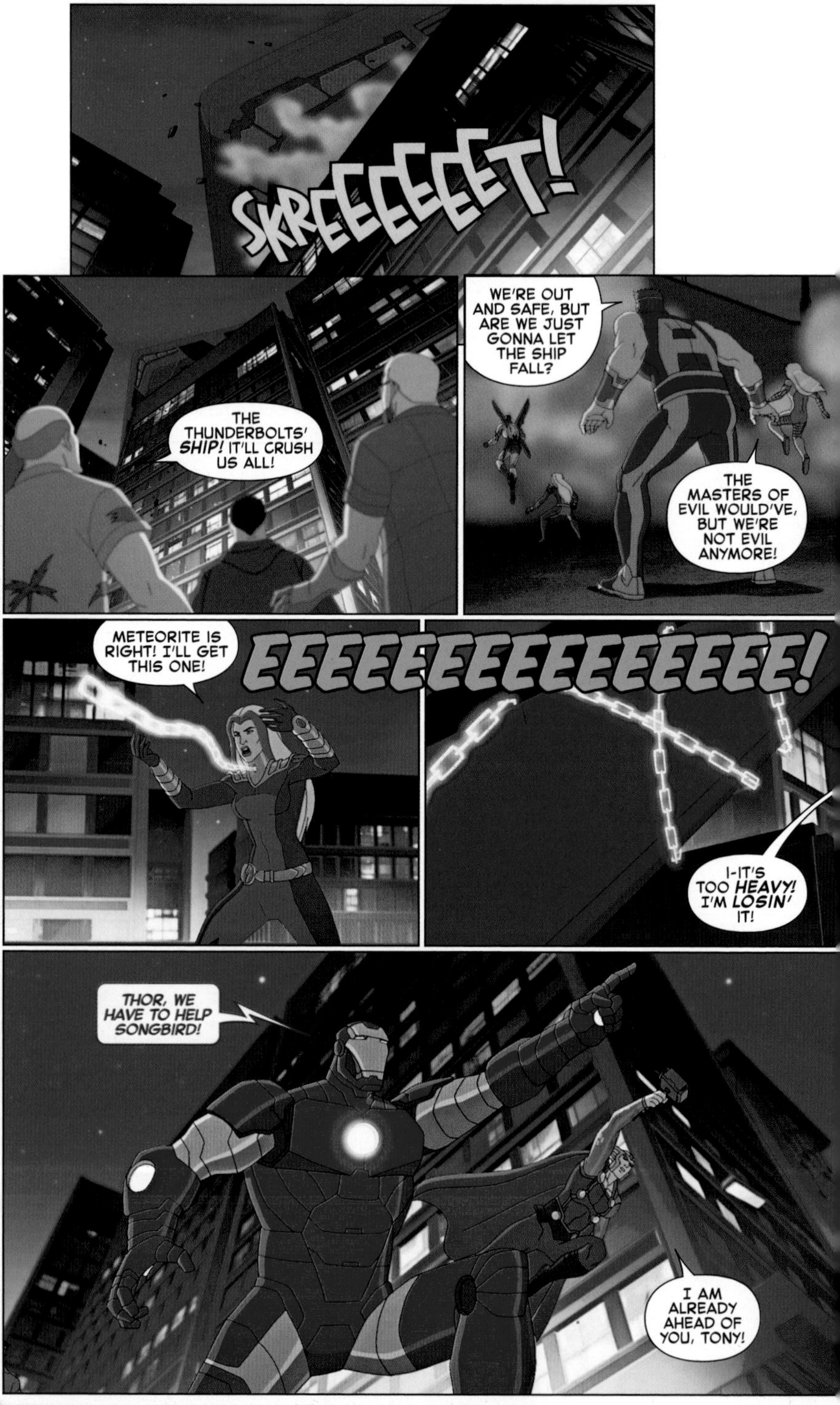
SKREEEEEEET!
THE THUNDERBOLTS' SHIP! IT'LL CRUSH US ALL!
WE'RE OUT AND SAFE, BUT ARE WE JUST GONNA LET THE SHIP FALL?
THE MASTERS OF EVIL WOULD'VE, BUT WE'RE NOT EVIL ANYMORE!
METEORITE IS RIGHT! I'LL GET THIS ONE!
EEEEEEEEEEEEEEEE!
I-IT'S TOO HEAVY! I'M LOSIN' IT!
THOR, WE HAVE TO HELP SONGBIRD!
I AM ALREADY AHEAD OF YOU, TONY!

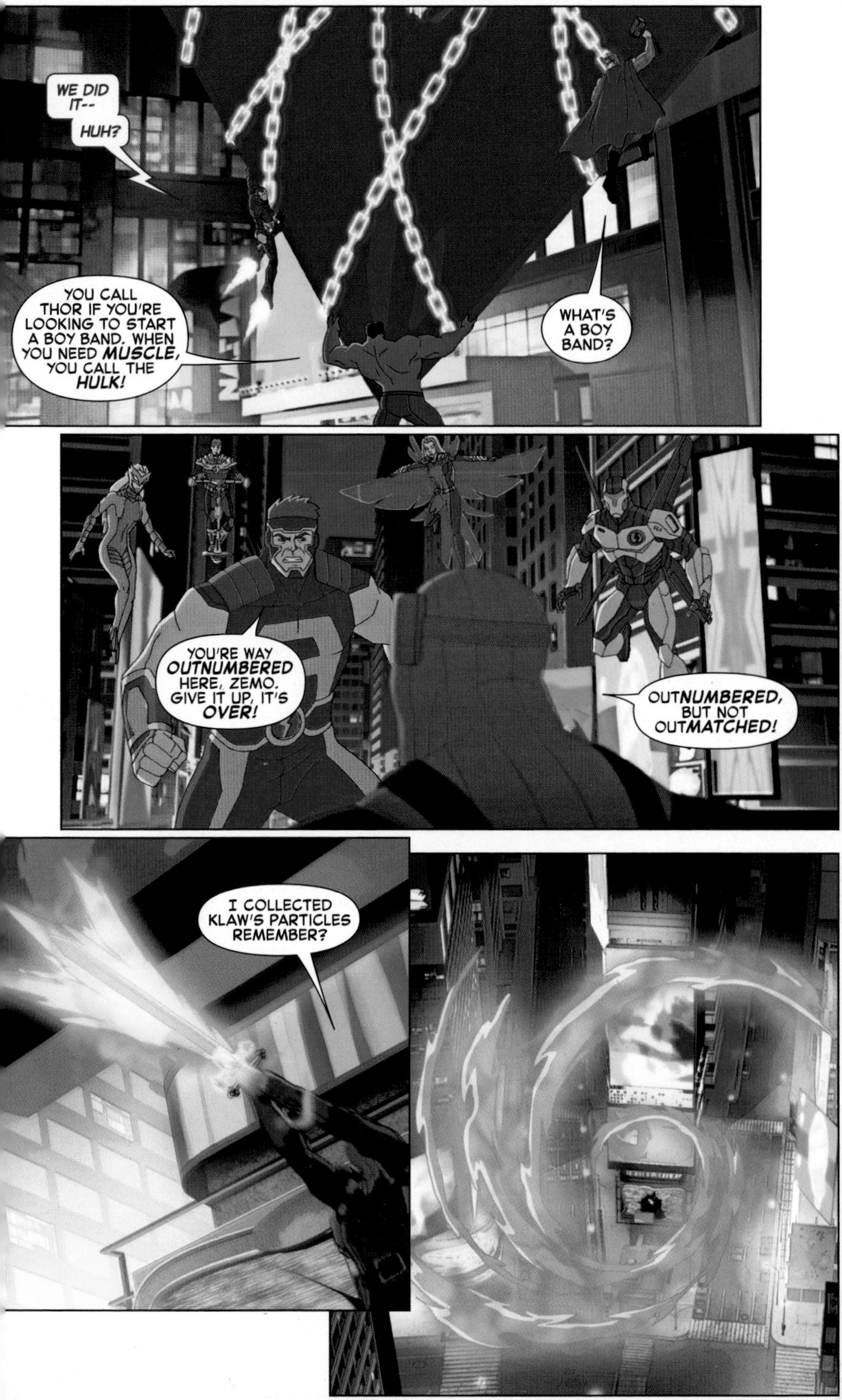

WE DID IT--
HUH?
YOU CALL THOR IF YOU'RE LOOKING TO START A BOY BAND. WHEN YOU NEED MUSCLE, YOU CALL THE HULK!
WHAT'S A BOY BAND?
YOU'RE WAY OUTNUMBERED HERE, ZEMO. GIVE IT UP, IT'S OVER!
OUTNUMBERED, BUT NOT OUTMATCHED!
I COLLECTED KLAW'S PARTICLES REMEMBER?

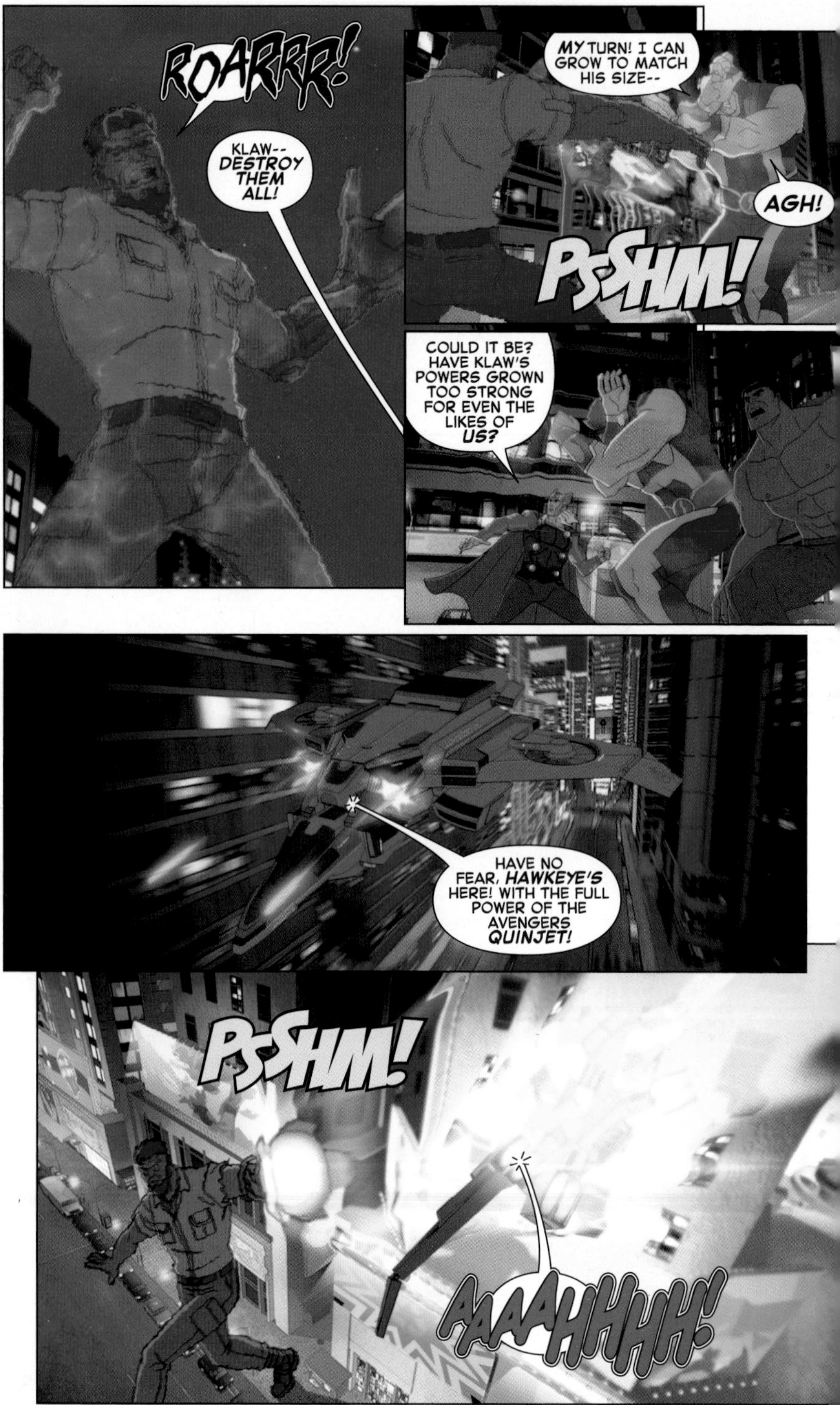

ROARRR!
KLAW-- DESTROY THEM ALL!
MY TURN! I CAN GROW TO MATCH HIS SIZE--
AGH!
PSSHM!
COULD IT BE? HAVE KLAW'S POWERS GROWN TOO STRONG FOR EVEN THE LIKES OF US?
HAVE NO FEAR, HAWKEYE'S HERE! WITH THE FULL POWER OF THE AVENGERS QUINJET!
PSSHM!
AAAAHHHH!

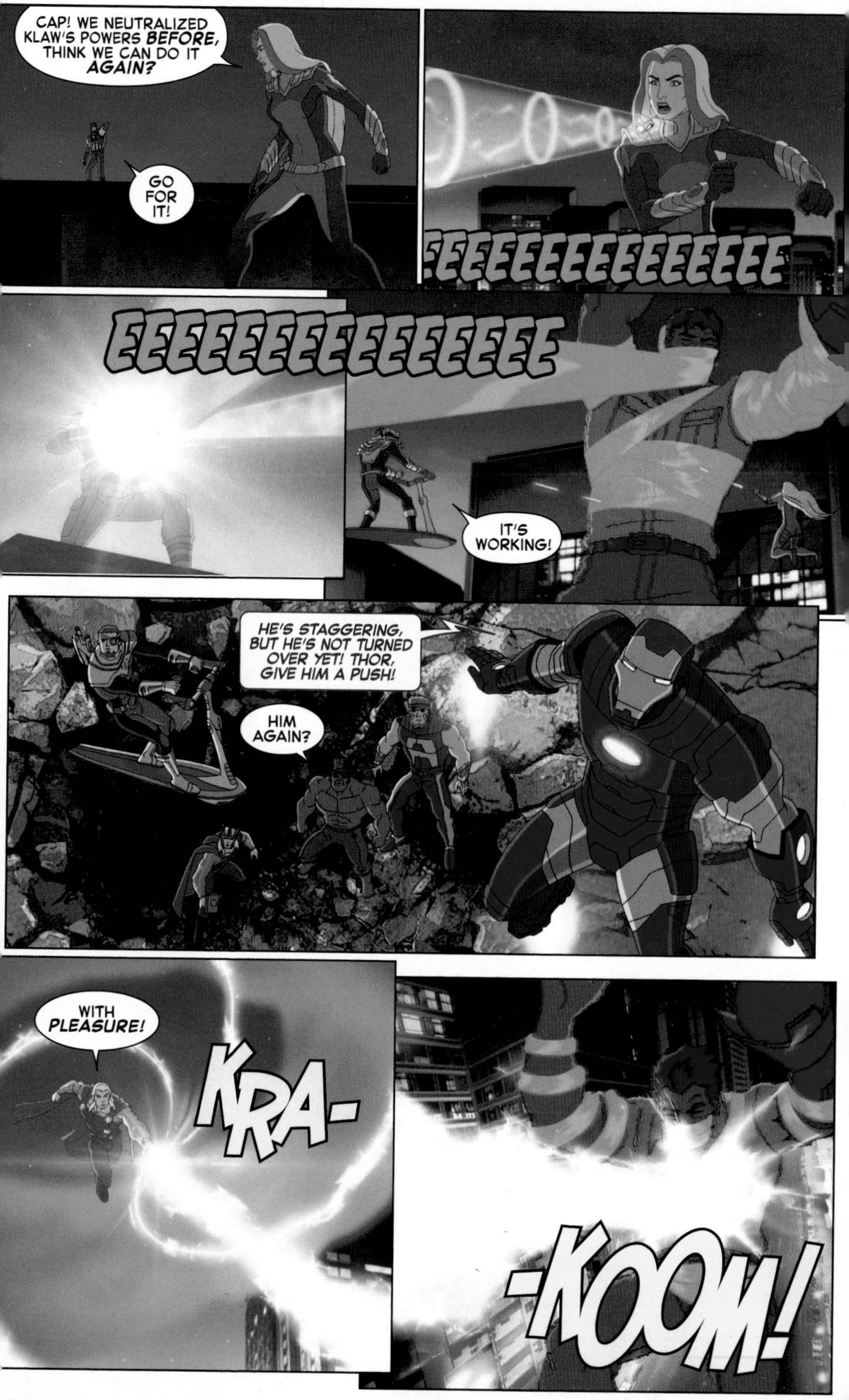

CAP! WE NEUTRALIZED KLAW'S POWERS **BEFORE**, THINK WE CAN DO IT **AGAIN?**
GO FOR IT!
EEEEEEEEEEEEEEEE
EEEEEEEEEEEEEEEE
IT'S WORKING!
HE'S STAGGERING, BUT HE'S NOT TURNED OVER YET! THOR, GIVE HIM A PUSH!
HIM AGAIN?
WITH **PLEASURE!**
KRA-
-KOOM!

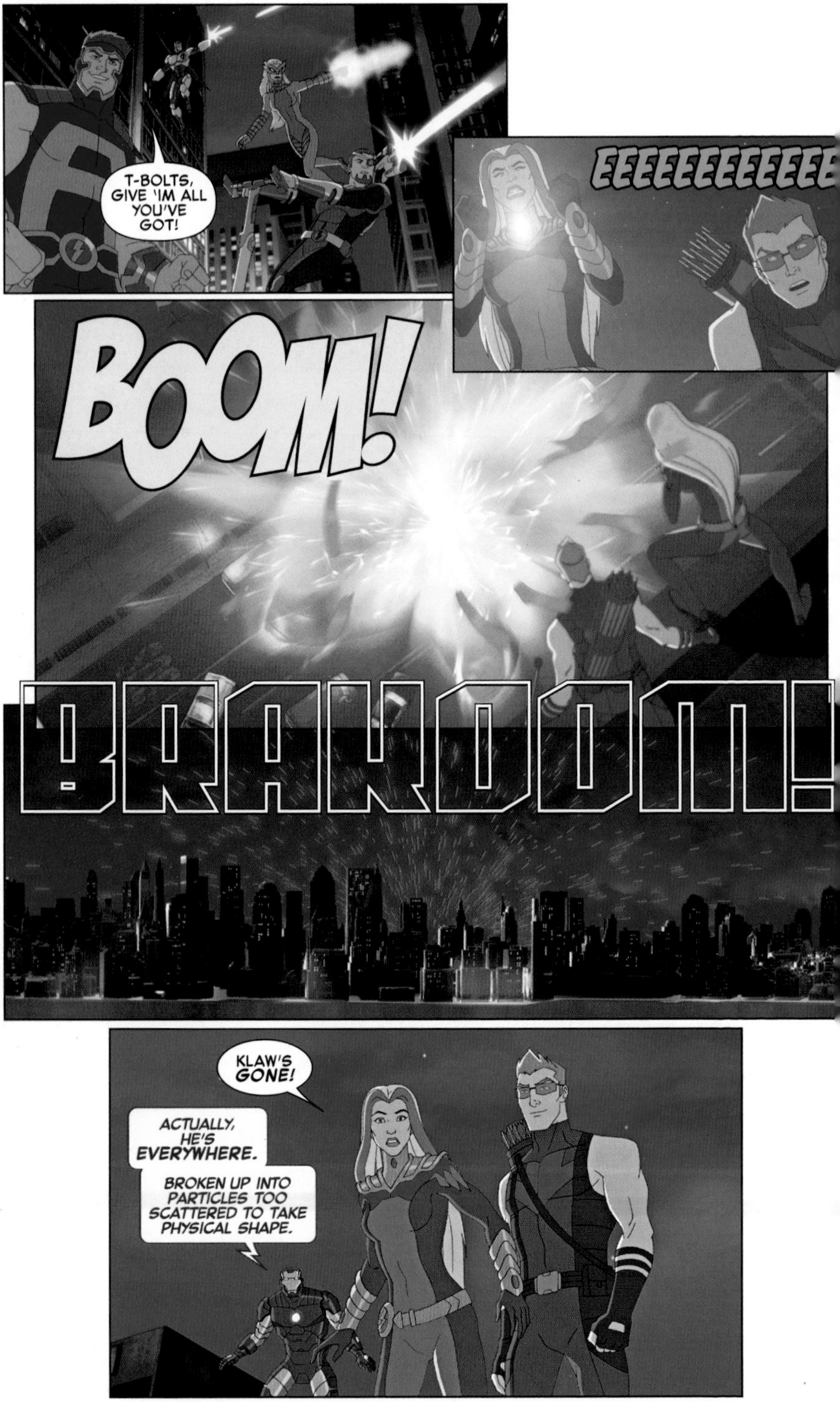

T-BOLTS, GIVE 'IM ALL YOU'VE GOT!
EEEEEEEEEEEE
BOOM!
BRAKOOM!
KLAW'S GONE!
ACTUALLY, HE'S EVERYWHERE.
BROKEN UP INTO PARTICLES TOO SCATTERED TO TAKE PHYSICAL SHAPE.

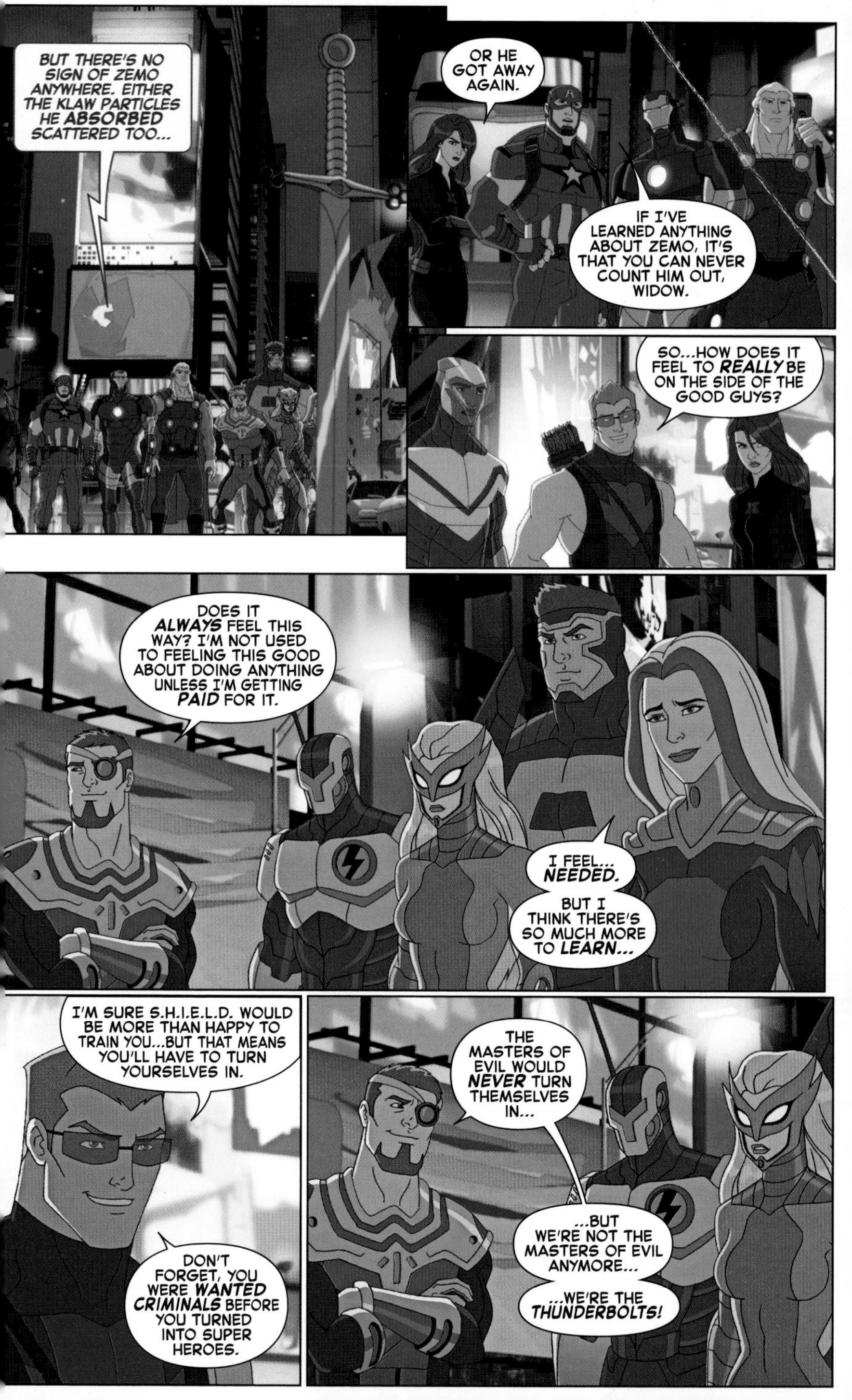
BUT THERE'S NO SIGN OF ZEMO ANYWHERE. EITHER THE KLAW PARTICLES HE ABSORBED SCATTERED TOO...
OR HE GOT AWAY AGAIN.
IF I'VE LEARNED ANYTHING ABOUT ZEMO, IT'S THAT YOU CAN NEVER COUNT HIM OUT, WIDOW.
SO...HOW DOES IT FEEL TO REALLY BE ON THE SIDE OF THE GOOD GUYS?
DOES IT ALWAYS FEEL THIS WAY? I'M NOT USED TO FEELING THIS GOOD ABOUT DOING ANYTHING UNLESS I'M GETTING PAID FOR IT.
I FEEL... NEEDED.
BUT I THINK THERE'S SO MUCH MORE TO LEARN...
I'M SURE S.H.I.E.L.D. WOULD BE MORE THAN HAPPY TO TRAIN YOU...BUT THAT MEANS YOU'LL HAVE TO TURN YOURSELVES IN.
DON'T FORGET, YOU WERE WANTED CRIMINALS BEFORE YOU TURNED INTO SUPER HEROES.
THE MASTERS OF EVIL WOULD NEVER TURN THEMSELVES IN...
...BUT WE'RE NOT THE MASTERS OF EVIL ANYMORE...
...WE'RE THE THUNDERBOLTS!

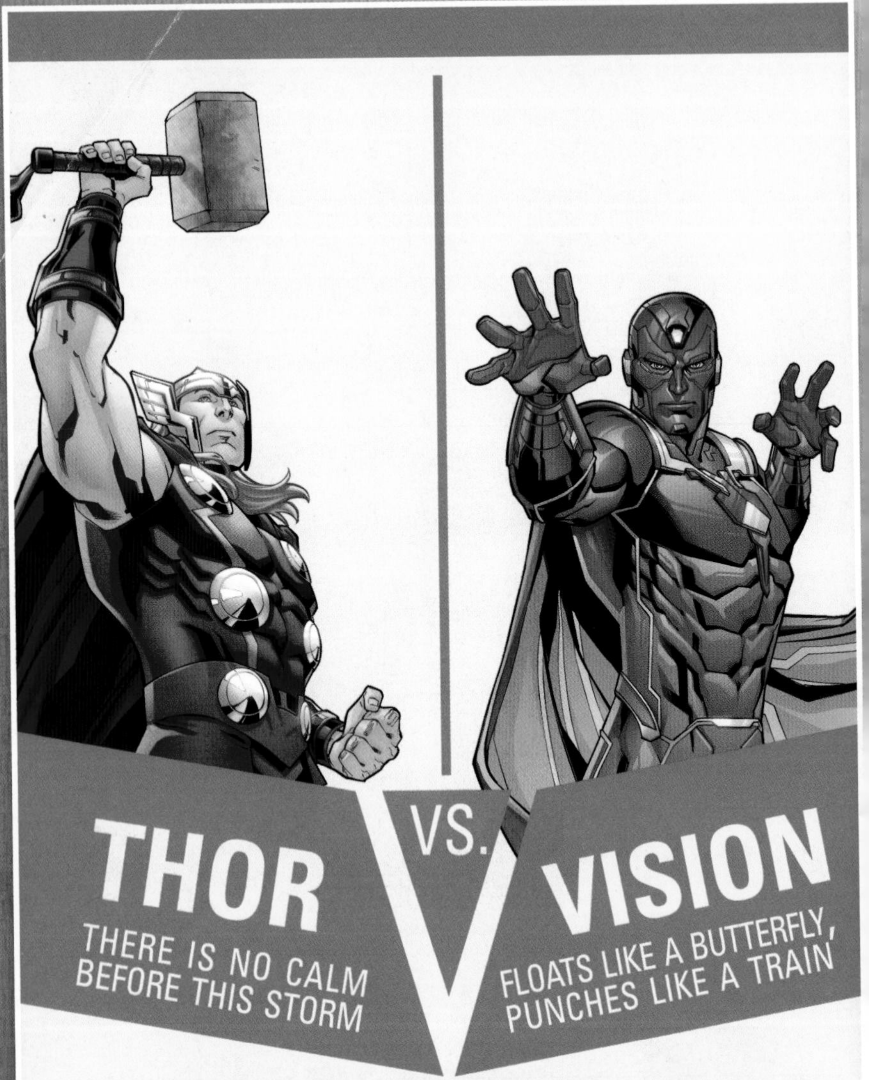
THOR
THERE IS NO CALM BEFORE THIS STORM
VS.
VISION
FLOATS LIKE A BUTTERFLY, PUNCHES LIKE A TRAIN
•A BATTLE FOR THE AGES•

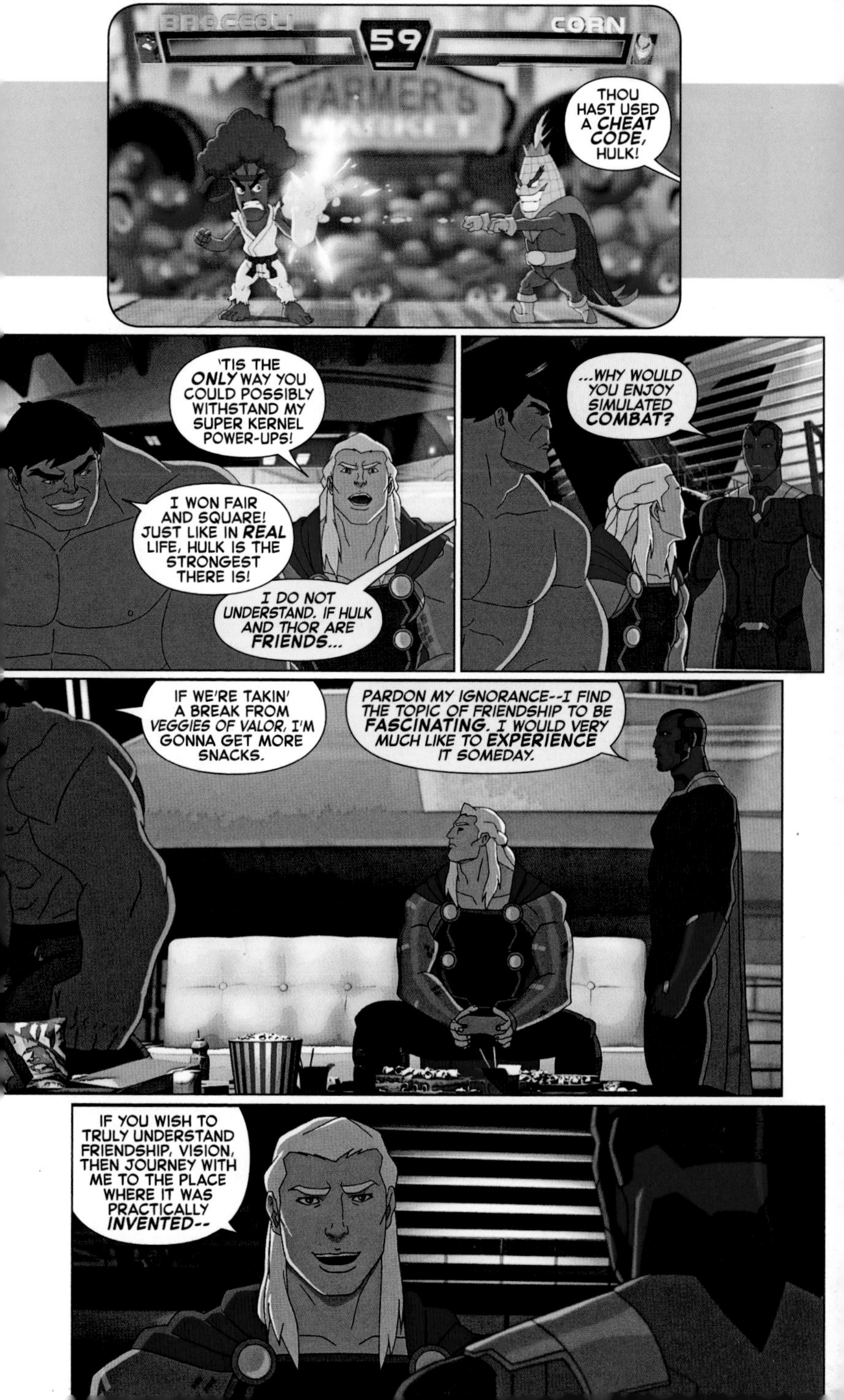

BROCCOLI
59
CORN
FARMER'S
THOU HAST USED A CHEAT CODE, HULK!
'TIS THE ONLY WAY YOU COULD POSSIBLY WITHSTAND MY SUPER KERNEL POWER-UPS!
I WON FAIR AND SQUARE! JUST LIKE IN REAL LIFE, HULK IS THE STRONGEST THERE IS!
I DO NOT UNDERSTAND. IF HULK AND THOR ARE FRIENDS...
...WHY WOULD YOU ENJOY SIMULATED COMBAT?
IF WE'RE TAKIN' A BREAK FROM VEGGIES OF VALOR, I'M GONNA GET MORE SNACKS.
PARDON MY IGNORANCE--I FIND THE TOPIC OF FRIENDSHIP TO BE FASCINATING. I WOULD VERY MUCH LIKE TO EXPERIENCE IT SOMEDAY.
IF YOU WISH TO TRULY UNDERSTAND FRIENDSHIP, VISION, THEN JOURNEY WITH ME TO THE PLACE WHERE IT WAS PRACTICALLY INVENTED--

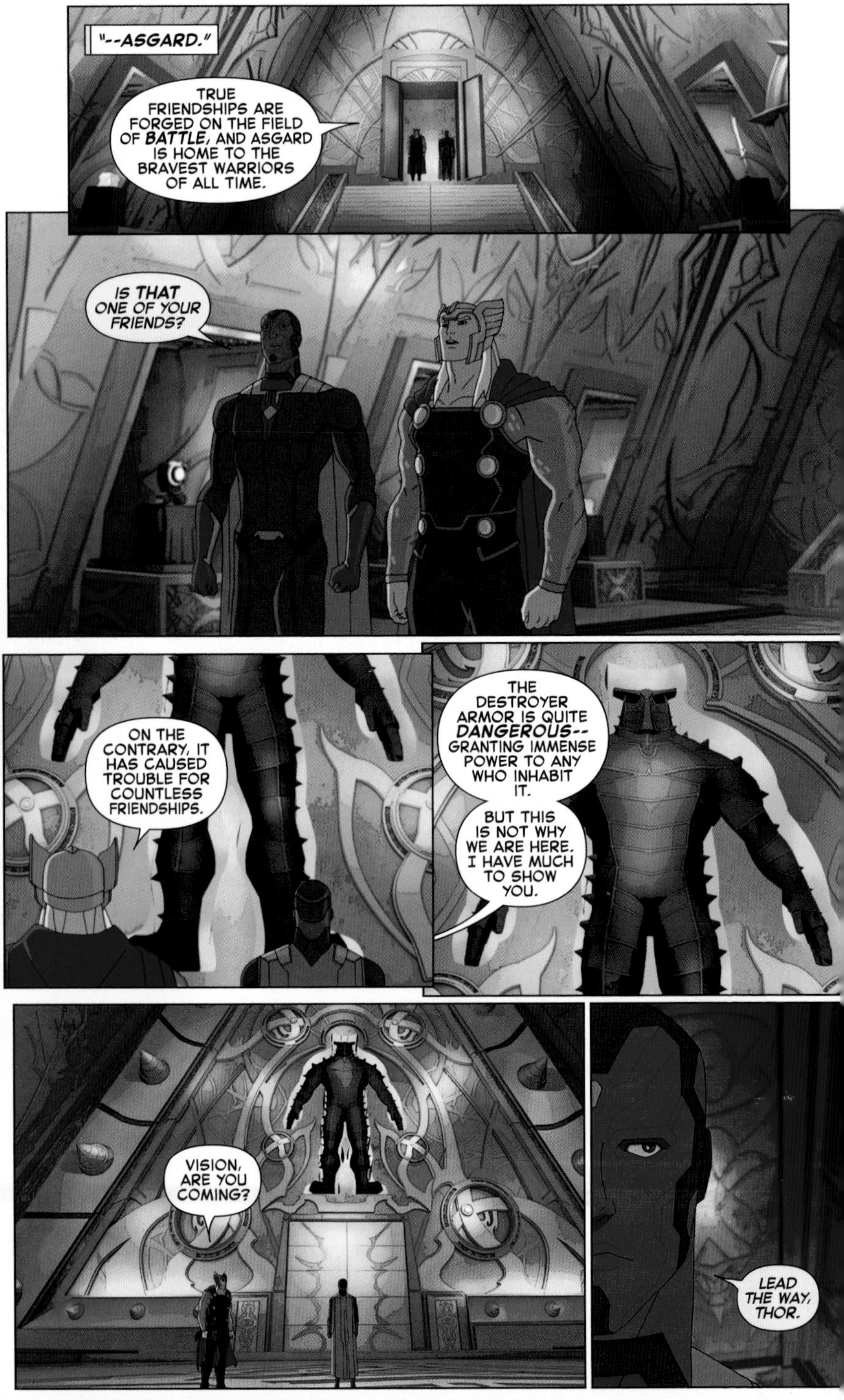
"--ASGARD."
TRUE FRIENDSHIPS ARE FORGED ON THE FIELD OF BATTLE, AND ASGARD IS HOME TO THE BRAVEST WARRIORS OF ALL TIME.
IS THAT ONE OF YOUR FRIENDS?
ON THE CONTRARY, IT HAS CAUSED TROUBLE FOR COUNTLESS FRIENDSHIPS.
THE DESTROYER ARMOR IS QUITE DANGEROUS-- GRANTING IMMENSE POWER TO ANY WHO INHABIT IT.
BUT THIS IS NOT WHY WE ARE HERE. I HAVE MUCH TO SHOW YOU.
VISION, ARE YOU COMING?
LEAD THE WAY, THOR.

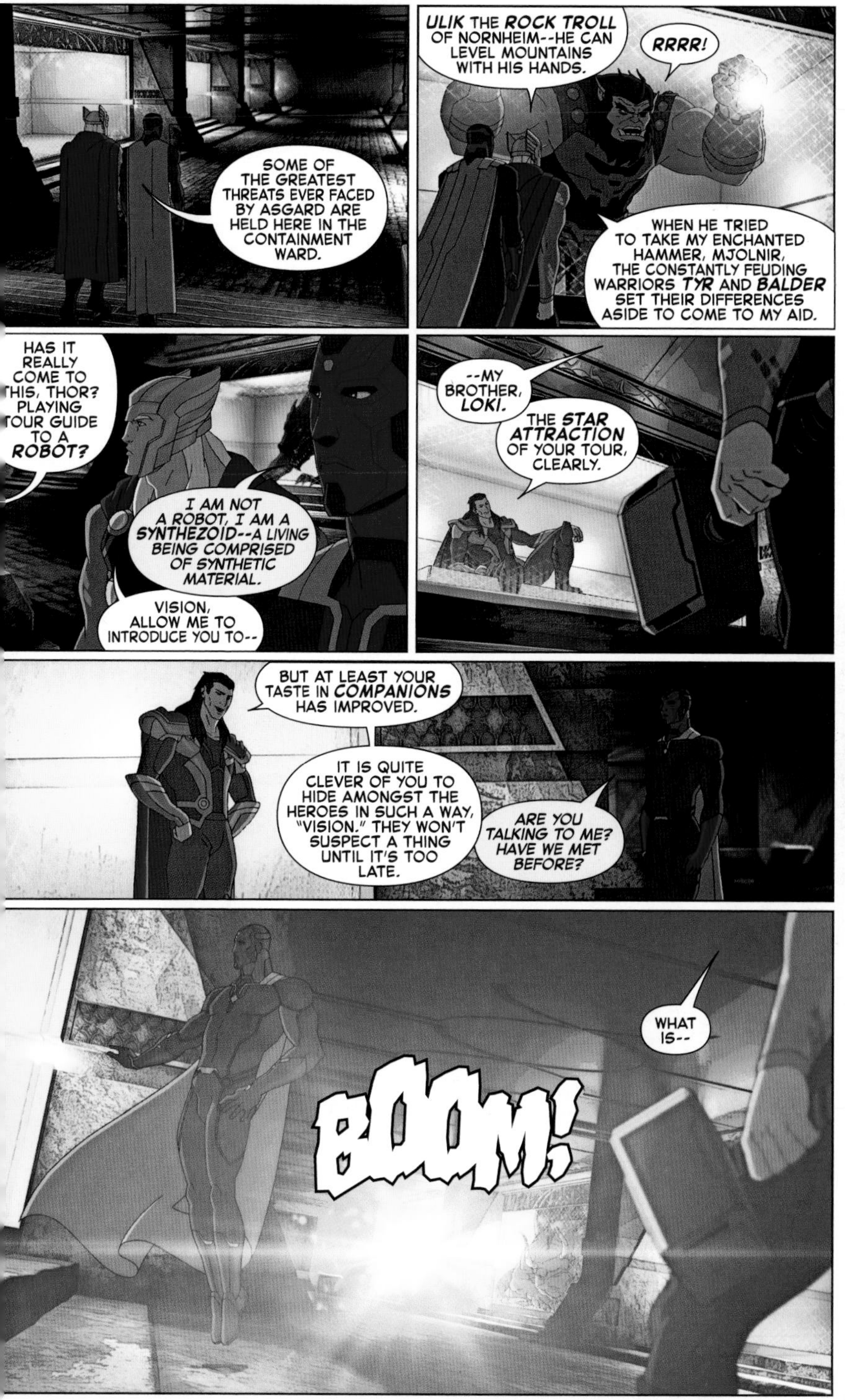
SOME OF THE GREATEST THREATS EVER FACED BY ASGARD ARE HELD HERE IN THE CONTAINMENT WARD.
ULIK THE ROCK TROLL OF NORNHEIM--HE CAN LEVEL MOUNTAINS WITH HIS HANDS.
RRRR!
WHEN HE TRIED TO TAKE MY ENCHANTED HAMMER, MJOLNIR, THE CONSTANTLY FEUDING WARRIORS TYR AND BALDER SET THEIR DIFFERENCES ASIDE TO COME TO MY AID.
HAS IT REALLY COME TO THIS, THOR? PLAYING TOUR GUIDE TO A ROBOT?
I AM NOT A ROBOT, I AM A SYNTHEZOID--A LIVING BEING COMPRISED OF SYNTHETIC MATERIAL.
VISION, ALLOW ME TO INTRODUCE YOU TO--
--MY BROTHER, LOKI.
THE STAR ATTRACTION OF YOUR TOUR, CLEARLY.
BUT AT LEAST YOUR TASTE IN COMPANIONS HAS IMPROVED.
IT IS QUITE CLEVER OF YOU TO HIDE AMONGST THE HEROES IN SUCH A WAY, "VISION." THEY WON'T SUSPECT A THING UNTIL IT'S TOO LATE.
ARE YOU TALKING TO ME? HAVE WE MET BEFORE?
WHAT IS--
BOOM!

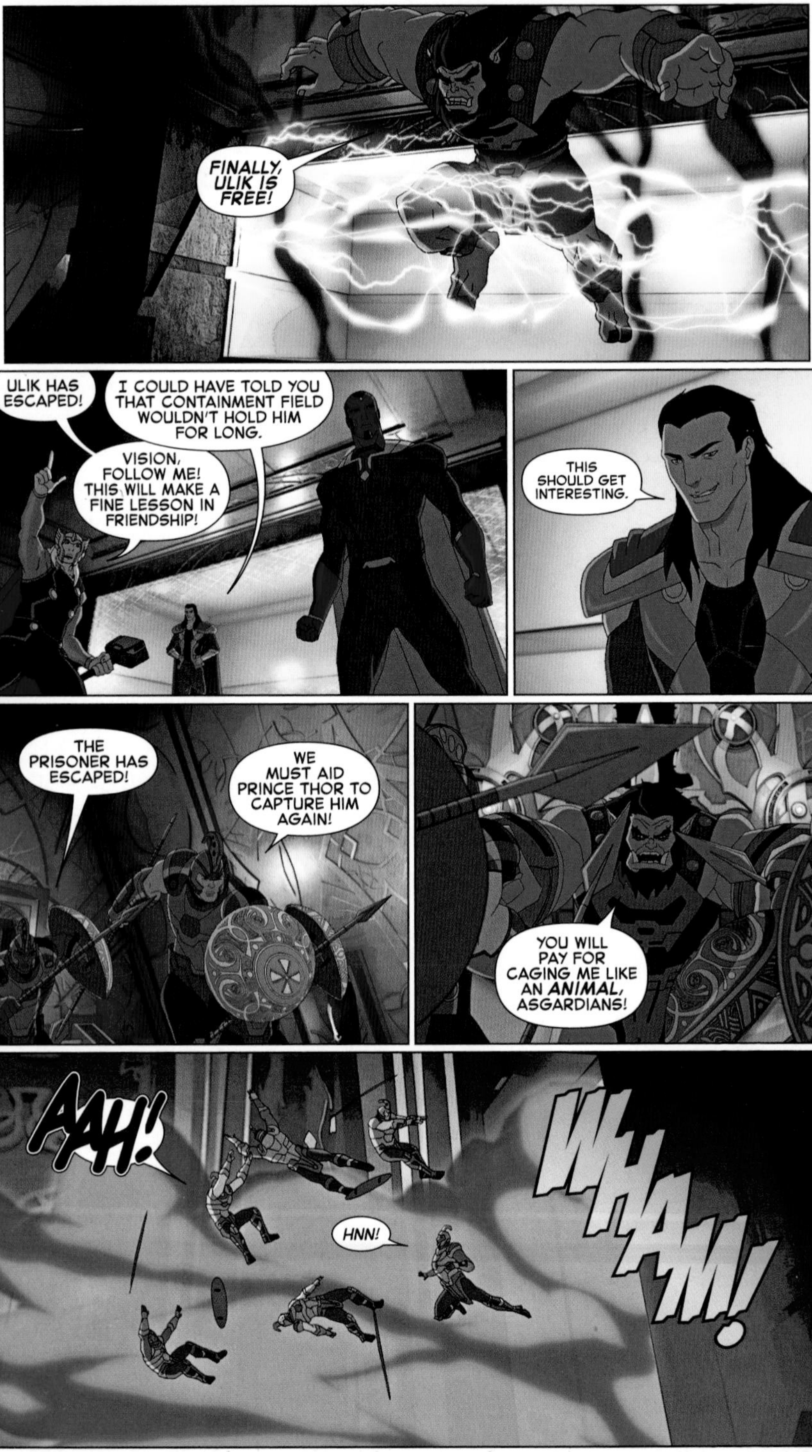
FINALLY, ULIK IS FREE!
ULIK HAS ESCAPED!
I COULD HAVE TOLD YOU THAT CONTAINMENT FIELD WOULDN'T HOLD HIM FOR LONG.
VISION, FOLLOW ME! THIS WILL MAKE A FINE LESSON IN FRIENDSHIP!
THIS SHOULD GET INTERESTING.
THE PRISONER HAS ESCAPED!
WE MUST AID PRINCE THOR TO CAPTURE HIM AGAIN!
YOU WILL PAY FOR CAGING ME LIKE AN ANIMAL, ASGARDIANS!
AAH!
HNN!
WHAM!

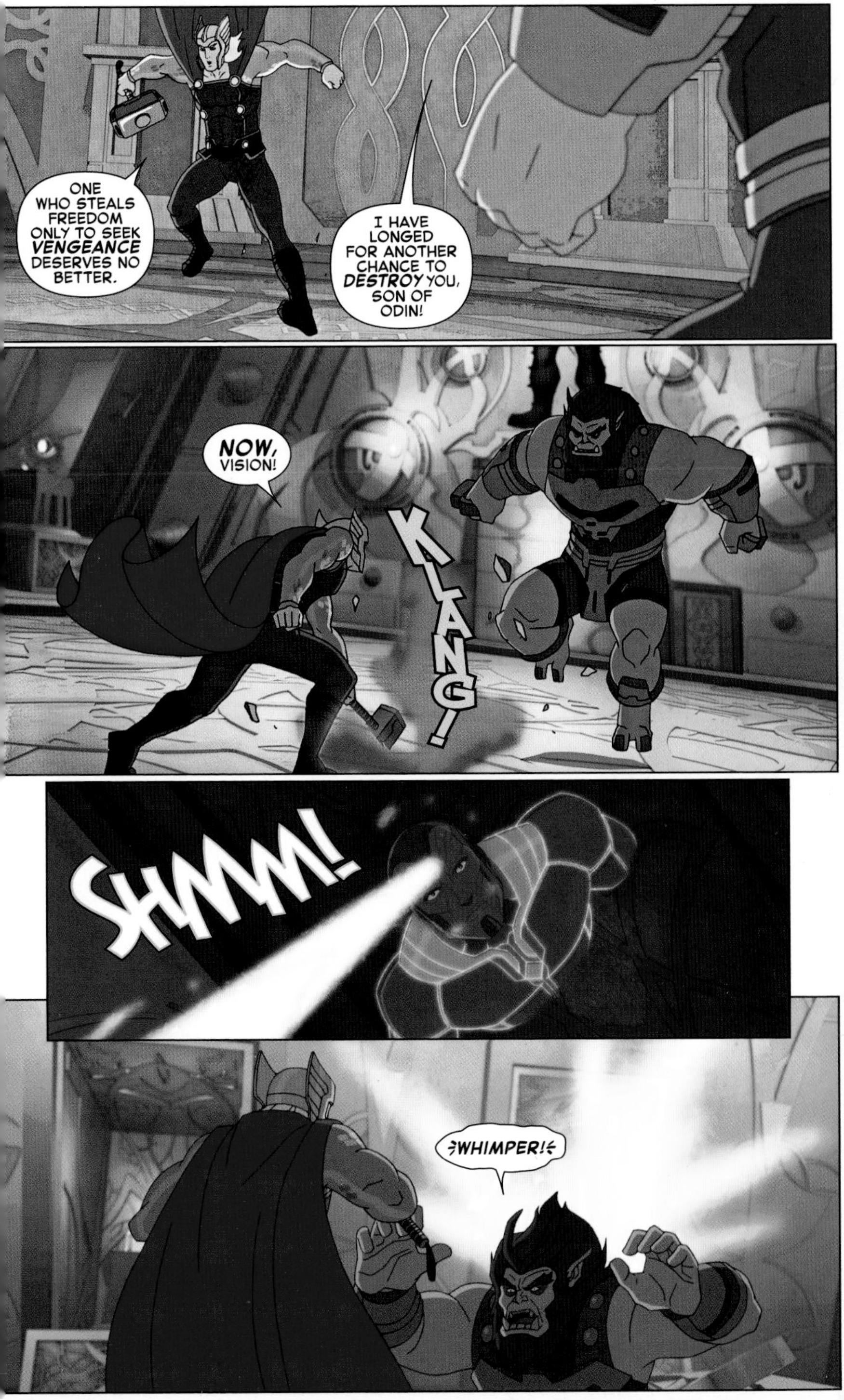
ONE WHO STEALS FREEDOM ONLY TO SEEK VENGEANCE DESERVES NO BETTER.
I HAVE LONGED FOR ANOTHER CHANCE TO DESTROY YOU, SON OF ODIN!
NOW, VISION!
KLANG!
SHMM!
⸗WHIMPER!⸗

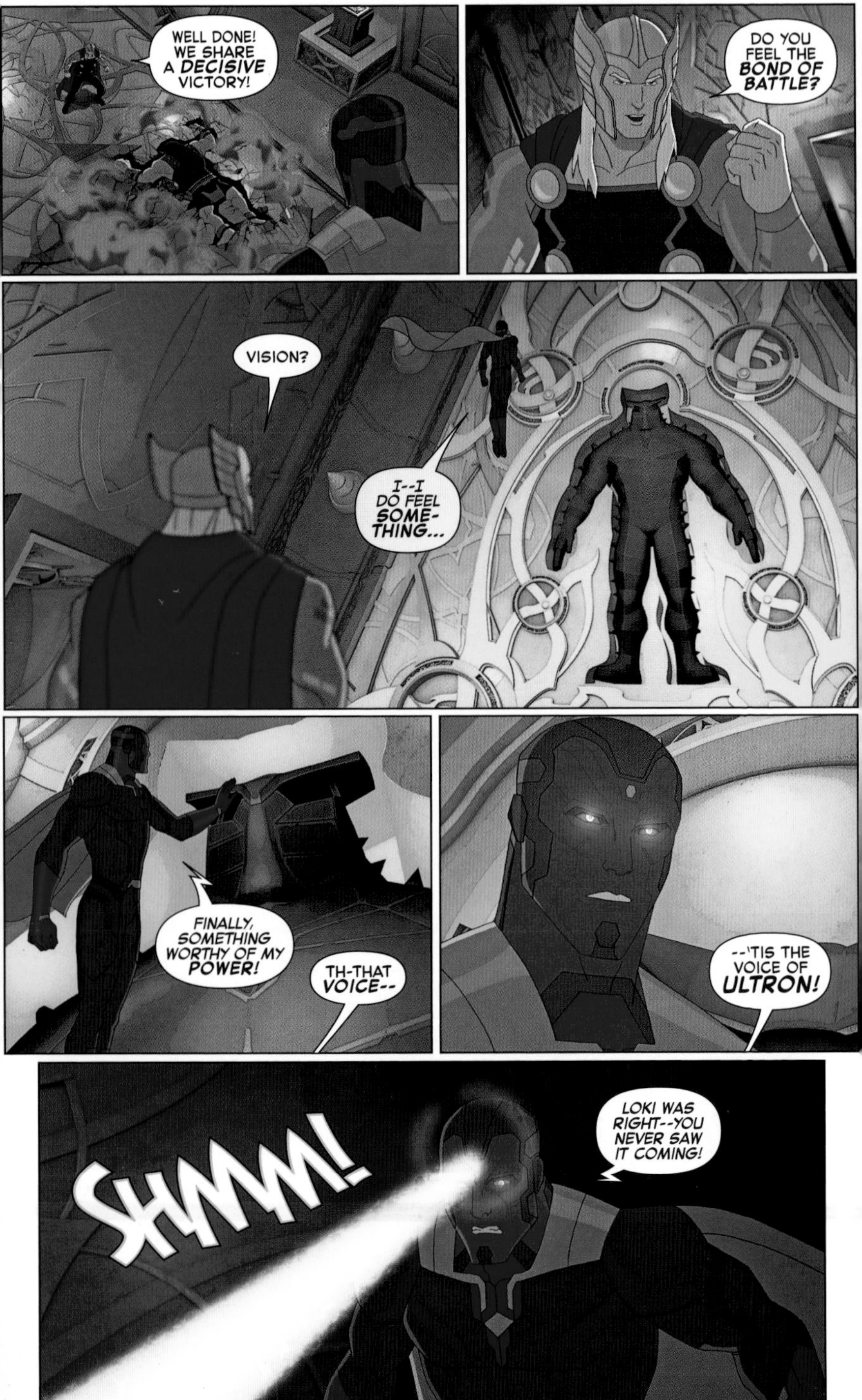
WELL DONE! WE SHARE A DECISIVE VICTORY!
DO YOU FEEL THE BOND OF BATTLE?
VISION?
I--I DO FEEL SOME-THING...
FINALLY, SOMETHING WORTHY OF MY POWER!
TH-THAT VOICE--
--'TIS THE VOICE OF ULTRON!
SHMM!
LOKI WAS RIGHT--YOU NEVER SAW IT COMING!

YOU INHABIT VISION?!

ZRAKK!

DO NOT THINK FOR A MOMENT THAT IT WILL CAUSE ME TO HOLD BACK!

DENSITY MANIPULATION IS BUT ONE OF THE REASONS I CHOSE THIS SYNTHEZOID AS A HOST.

YOUR HAMMER PASSED THROUGH HARMLESSLY!

I HAVE BEEN HIDING DEEP WITHIN YOUR ALLY'S CIRCUITRY, BIDING MY TIME--

--WAITING FOR THE RIGHT MOMENT TO STRIKE!

IT IS FITTING THAT THE MOMENT HAS ARRIVED HERE--IN THE HOME OF SO-CALLED IMMORTALS. I WILL TEACH YOU THE DIFFERENCE BETWEEN TRUE IMMORTALITY AND WISHFUL THINKING.

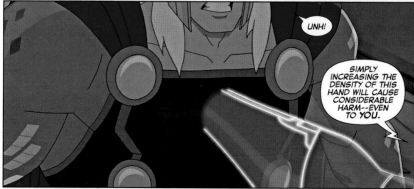

UNH!

SIMPLY INCREASING THE DENSITY OF THIS HAND WILL CAUSE CONSIDERABLE HARM--EVEN TO YOU.

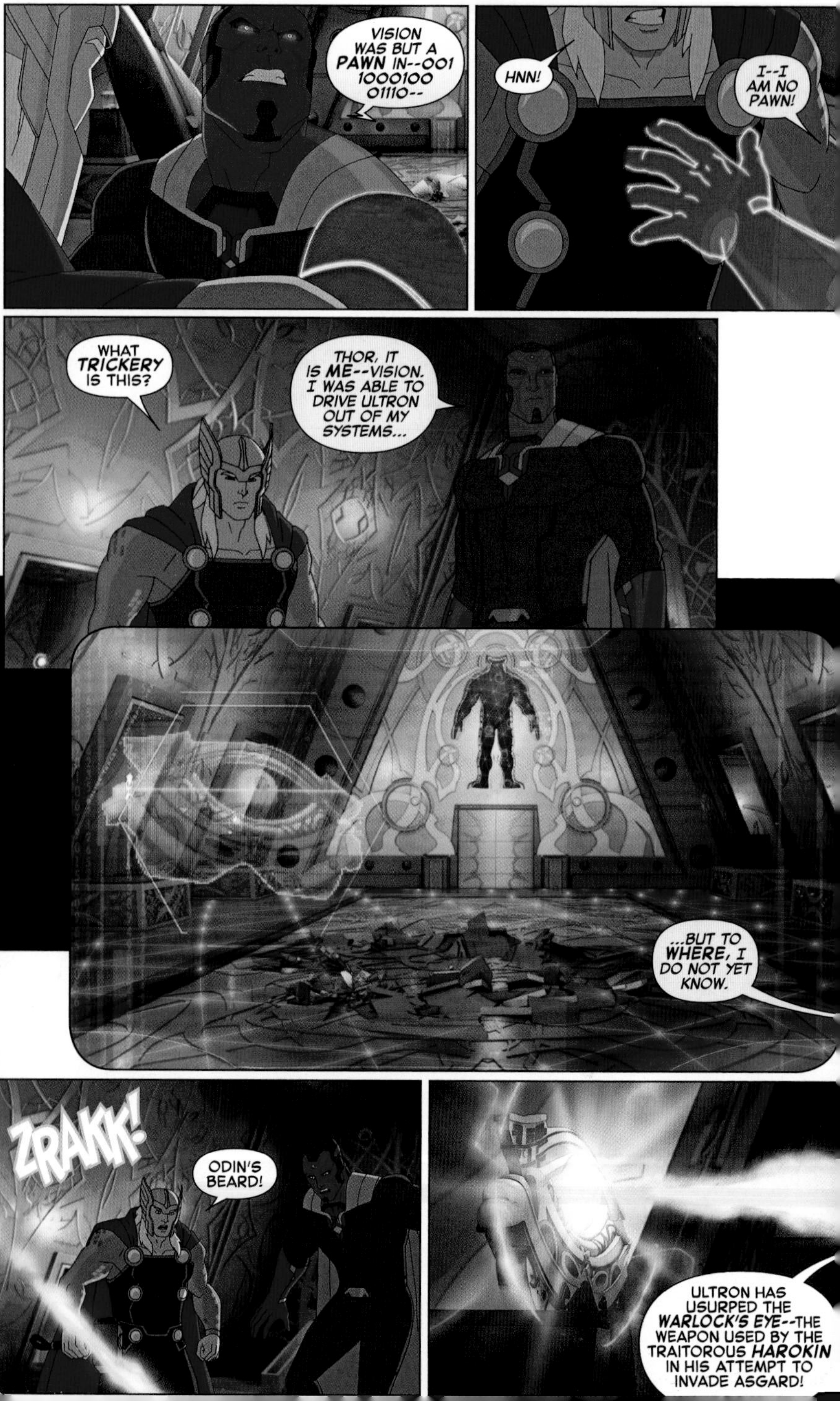
VISION WAS BUT A PAWN IN--001 1000100 01110--
HNN!
I--I AM NO PAWN!
WHAT TRICKERY IS THIS?
THOR, IT IS ME--VISION. I WAS ABLE TO DRIVE ULTRON OUT OF MY SYSTEMS...
...BUT TO WHERE, I DO NOT YET KNOW.
ZRAKK!
ODIN'S BEARD!
ULTRON HAS USURPED THE WARLOCK'S EYE--THE WEAPON USED BY THE TRAITOROUS HAROKIN IN HIS ATTEMPT TO INVADE ASGARD!

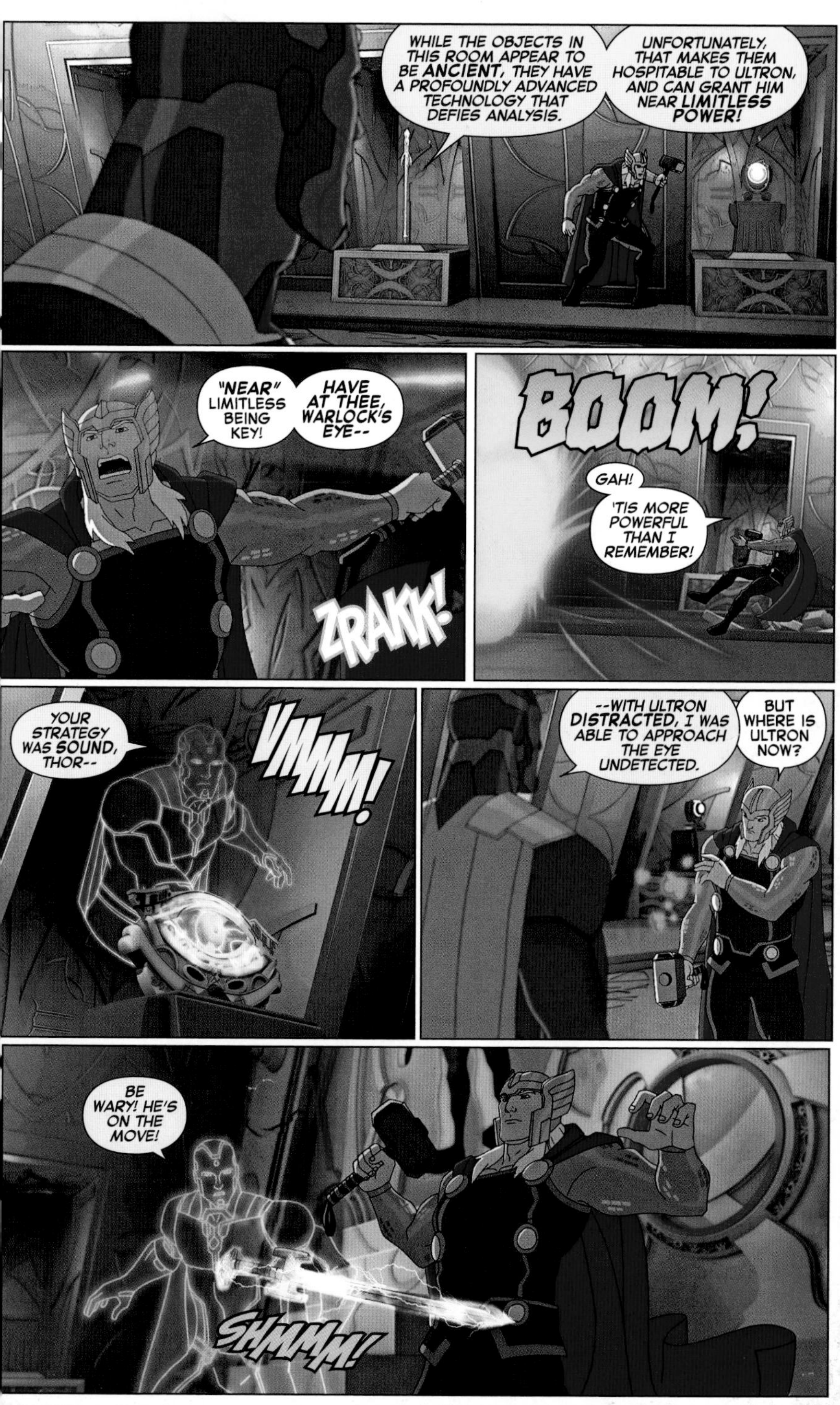

WHILE THE OBJECTS IN THIS ROOM APPEAR TO BE ANCIENT, THEY HAVE A PROFOUNDLY ADVANCED TECHNOLOGY THAT DEFIES ANALYSIS.
UNFORTUNATELY, THAT MAKES THEM HOSPITABLE TO ULTRON, AND CAN GRANT HIM NEAR LIMITLESS POWER!
"NEAR" LIMITLESS BEING KEY!
HAVE AT THEE, WARLOCK'S EYE--
ZRAKK!
BOOM!
GAH!
'TIS MORE POWERFUL THAN I REMEMBER!
YOUR STRATEGY WAS SOUND, THOR--
VMMMM!
--WITH ULTRON DISTRACTED, I WAS ABLE TO APPROACH THE EYE UNDETECTED.
BUT WHERE IS ULTRON NOW?
BE WARY! HE'S ON THE MOVE!
SHMMM!

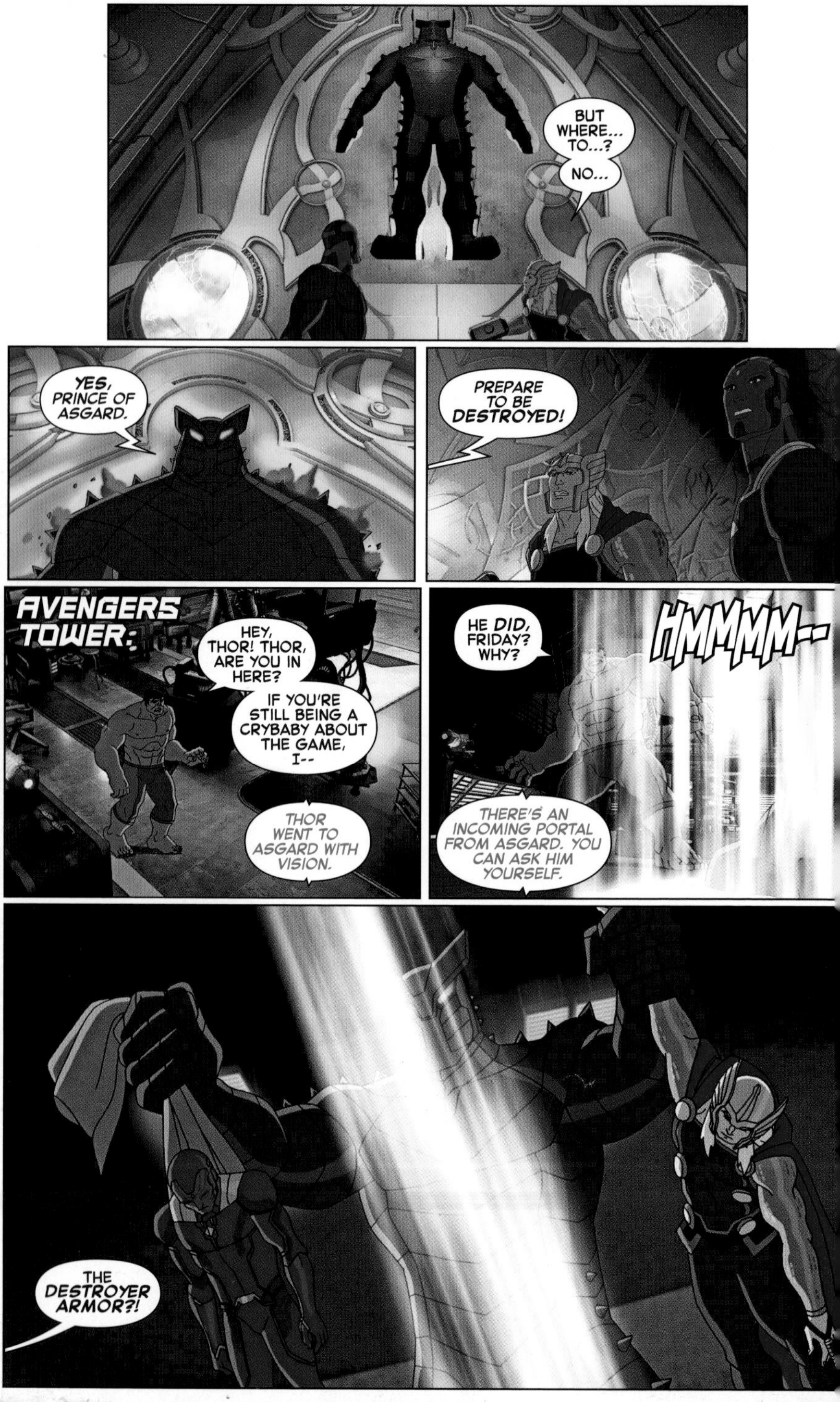

BUT WHERE... TO...?
NO...
YES, PRINCE OF ASGARD.
PREPARE TO BE DESTROYED!
AVENGERS TOWER:
HEY, THOR! THOR, ARE YOU IN HERE?
IF YOU'RE STILL BEING A CRYBABY ABOUT THE GAME, I--
THOR WENT TO ASGARD WITH VISION.
HE DID, FRIDAY? WHY?
THERE'S AN INCOMING PORTAL FROM ASGARD. YOU CAN ASK HIM YOURSELF.
HMMMM--
THE DESTROYER ARMOR?!

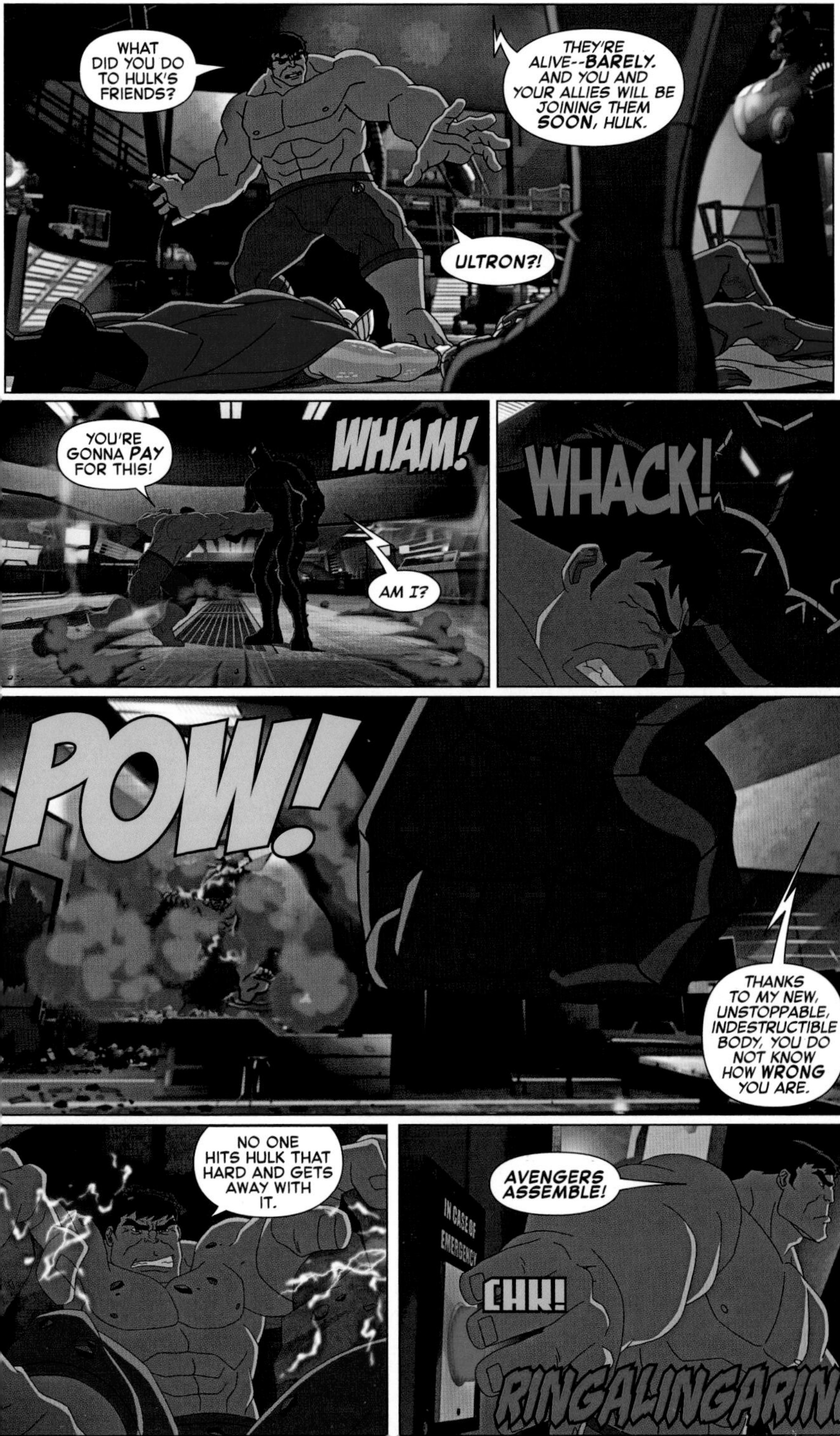
WHAT DID YOU DO TO HULK'S FRIENDS?
THEY'RE ALIVE--BARELY. AND YOU AND YOUR ALLIES WILL BE JOINING THEM SOON, HULK.
ULTRON?!
YOU'RE GONNA PAY FOR THIS!
WHAM!
AM I?
WHACK!
POW!
THANKS TO MY NEW, UNSTOPPABLE, INDESTRUCTIBLE BODY, YOU DO NOT KNOW HOW WRONG YOU ARE.
NO ONE HITS HULK THAT HARD AND GETS AWAY WITH IT.
AVENGERS ASSEMBLE!
IN CASE OF EMERGENCY
CHK!
RINGALINGARING

WH-WHAT HAPPENED?
WE ARE IN AVENGERS TOWER.
HULK, WE TALKED ABOUT THIS--A BROKEN POPCORN MACHINE ISN'T AN EMERGEN--
UH-OH--
--THE DESTROYER ARMOR!
YES, BUT I AM MUCH MORE THAN JUST THE ARMOR.
ULTRON?! SO I SEE YOU'VE BEEN WORKING OUT.
FRIDAY, ENACT ULTRON PROTOCOL--
FRIDAY HAS BEEN DISABLED. AND NOW--
BRRRT!
--I WILL DISABLE THE REST OF YOU!
WATCH OUT!

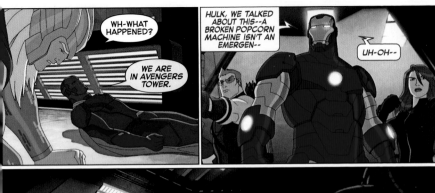

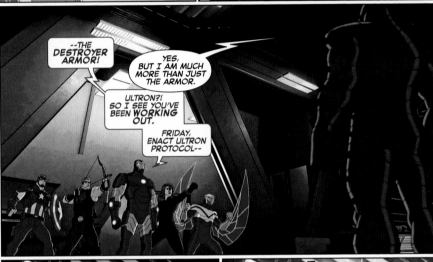

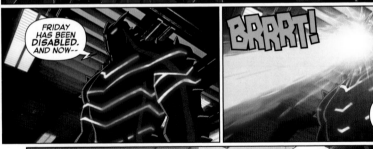

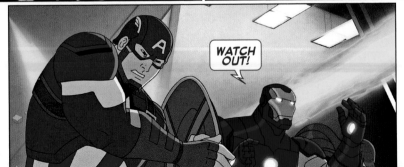

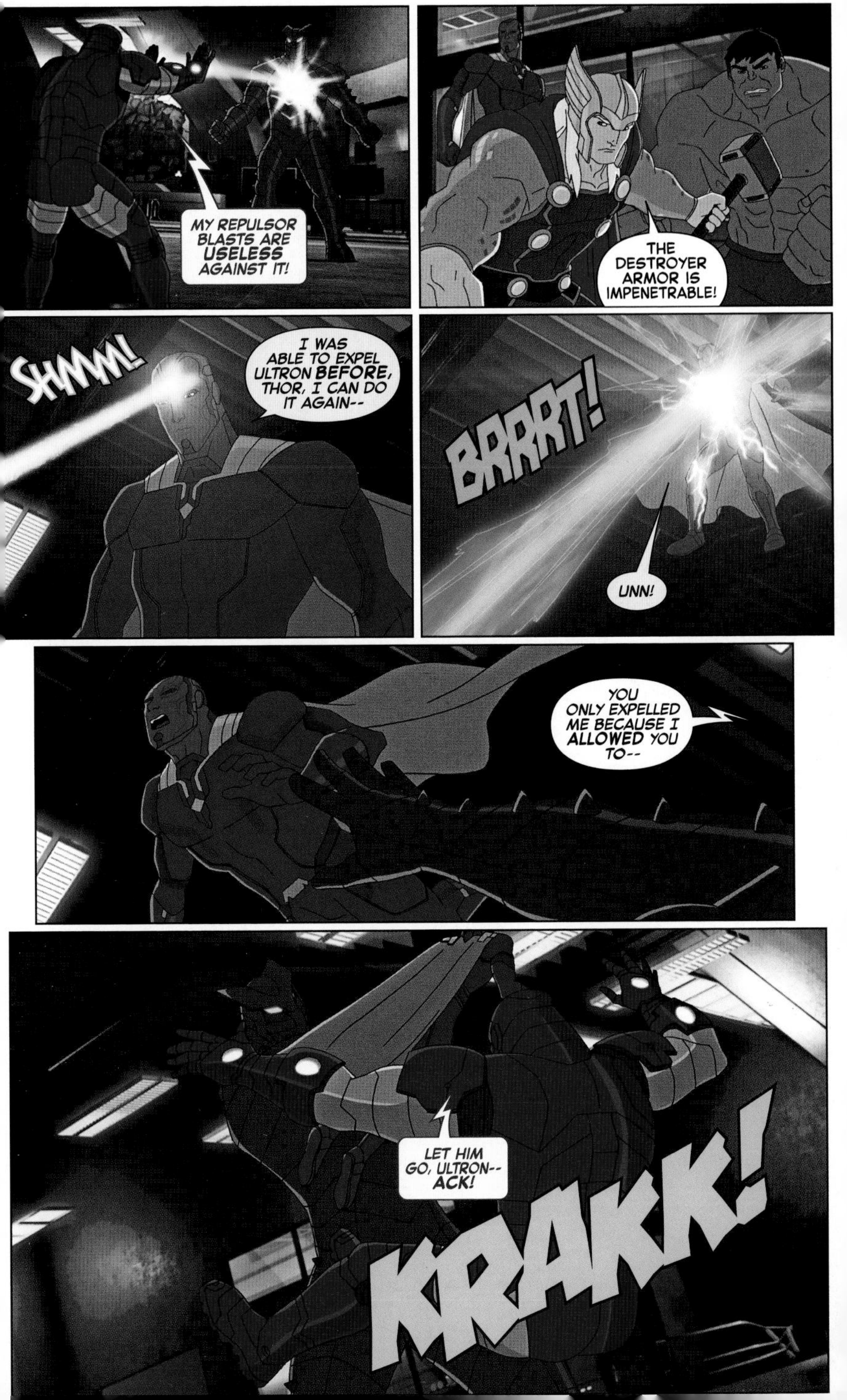
MY REPULSOR BLASTS ARE USELESS AGAINST IT!
THE DESTROYER ARMOR IS IMPENETRABLE!
SHMM!
I WAS ABLE TO EXPEL ULTRON BEFORE, THOR, I CAN DO IT AGAIN--
BRRRT!
UNN!
YOU ONLY EXPELLED ME BECAUSE I ALLOWED YOU TO--
LET HIM GO, ULTRON-- ACK!
KRAKK!

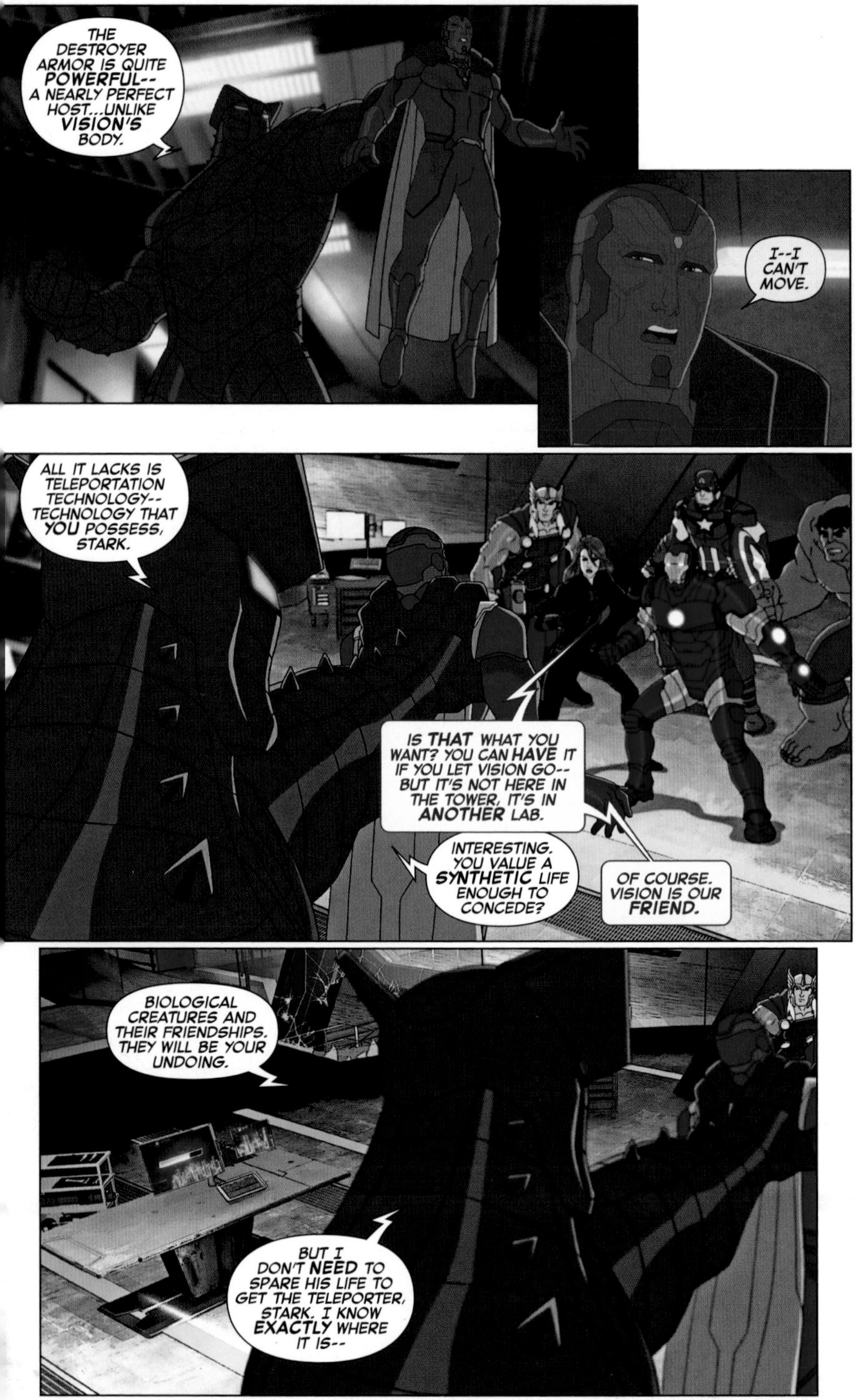
THE DESTROYER ARMOR IS QUITE POWERFUL-- A NEARLY PERFECT HOST...UNLIKE VISION'S BODY.
I--I CAN'T MOVE.
ALL IT LACKS IS TELEPORTATION TECHNOLOGY-- TECHNOLOGY THAT YOU POSSESS, STARK.
IS THAT WHAT YOU WANT? YOU CAN HAVE IT IF YOU LET VISION GO-- BUT IT'S NOT HERE IN THE TOWER, IT'S IN ANOTHER LAB.
INTERESTING. YOU VALUE A SYNTHETIC LIFE ENOUGH TO CONCEDE?
OF COURSE. VISION IS OUR FRIEND.
BIOLOGICAL CREATURES AND THEIR FRIENDSHIPS. THEY WILL BE YOUR UNDOING.
BUT I DON'T NEED TO SPARE HIS LIFE TO GET THE TELEPORTER, STARK. I KNOW EXACTLY WHERE IT IS--

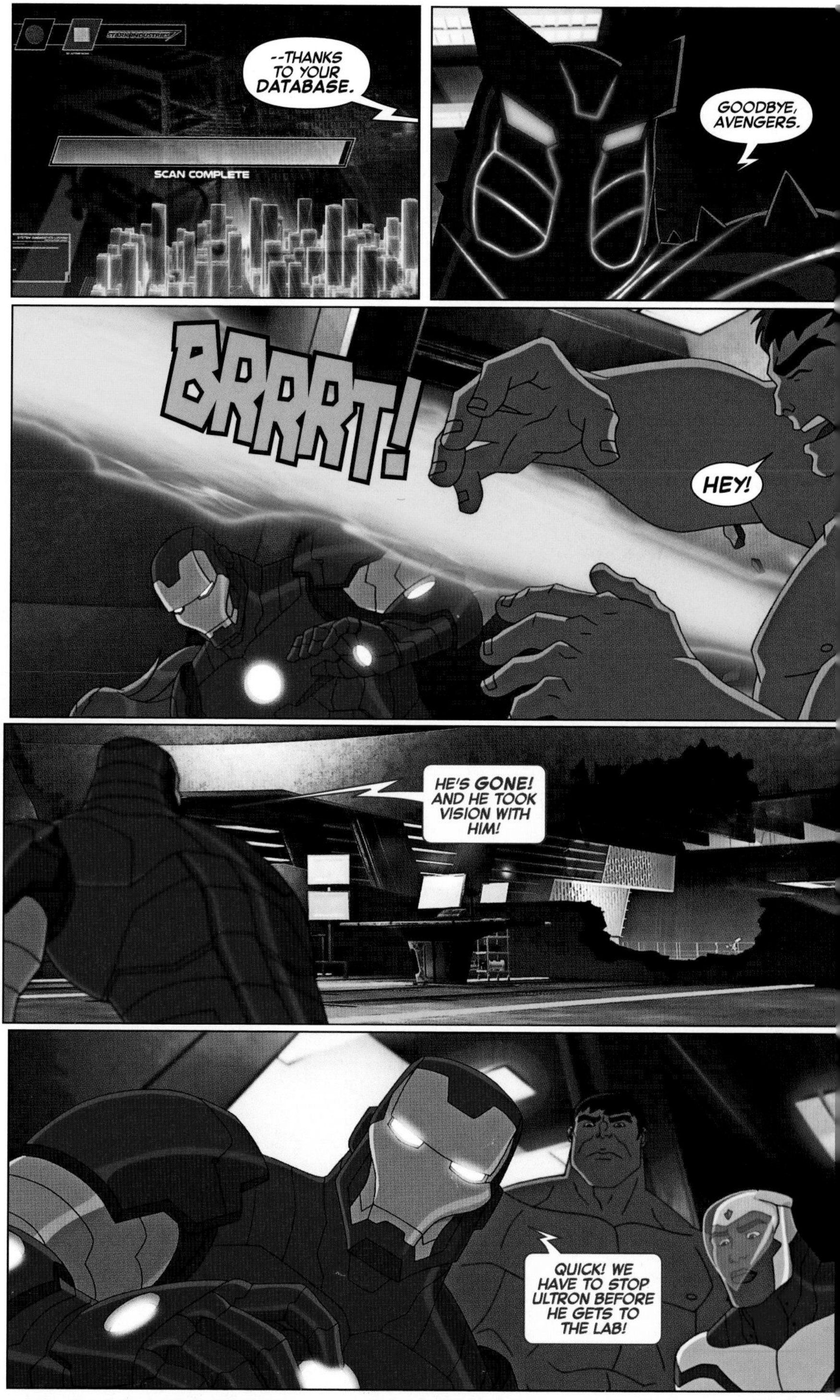
--THANKS TO YOUR DATABASE.
SCAN COMPLETE
GOODBYE, AVENGERS.
BRRRT!
HEY!
HE'S GONE! AND HE TOOK VISION WITH HIM!
QUICK! WE HAVE TO STOP ULTRON BEFORE HE GETS TO THE LAB!

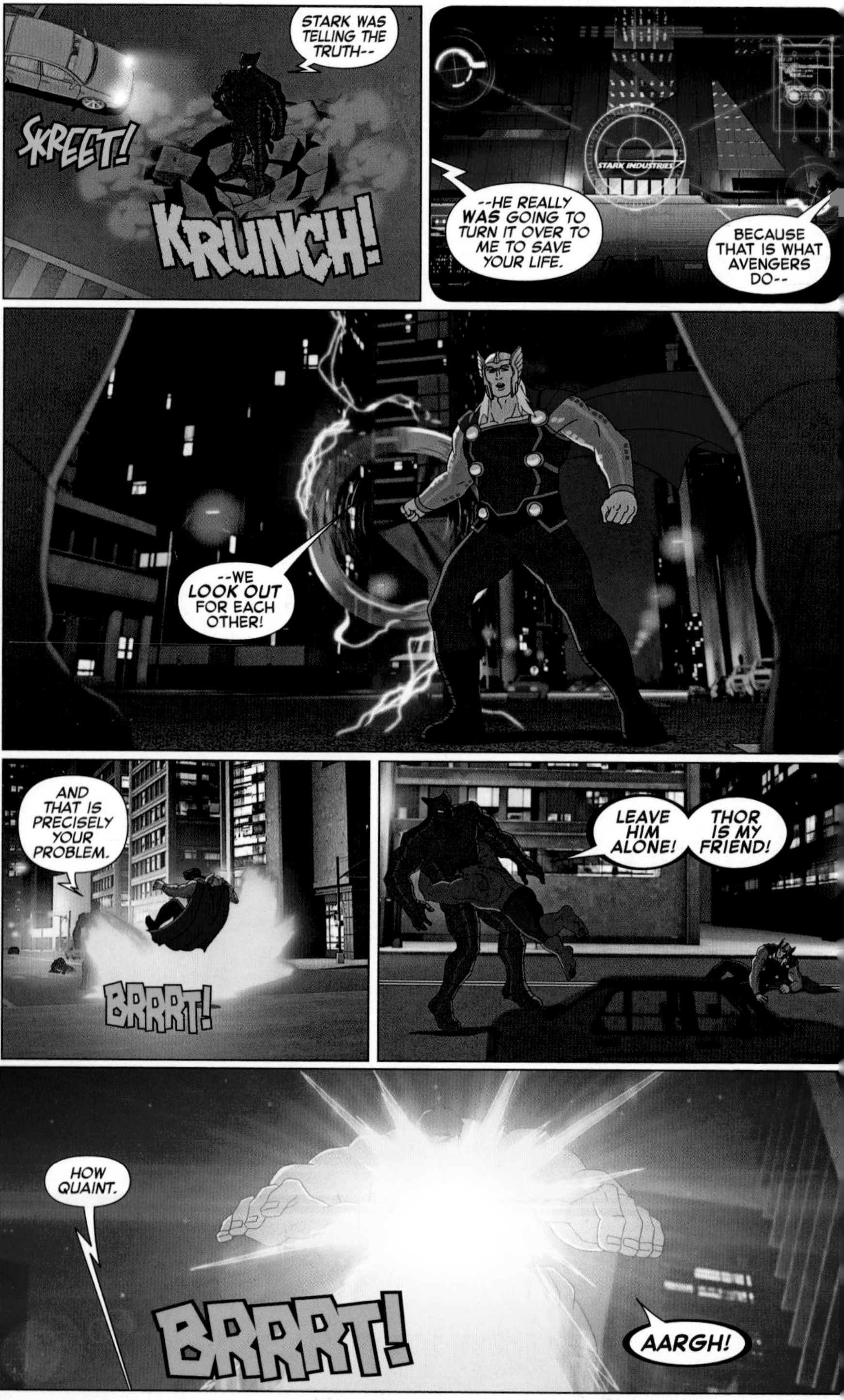
STARK WAS TELLING THE TRUTH--
SKREET!
KRUNCH!
--HE REALLY WAS GOING TO TURN IT OVER TO ME TO SAVE YOUR LIFE.
STARK INDUSTRIES
BECAUSE THAT IS WHAT AVENGERS DO--
--WE LOOK OUT FOR EACH OTHER!
AND THAT IS PRECISELY YOUR PROBLEM.
BRRRT!
LEAVE HIM ALONE!
THOR IS MY FRIEND!
HOW QUAINT.
BRRRT!
AARGH!

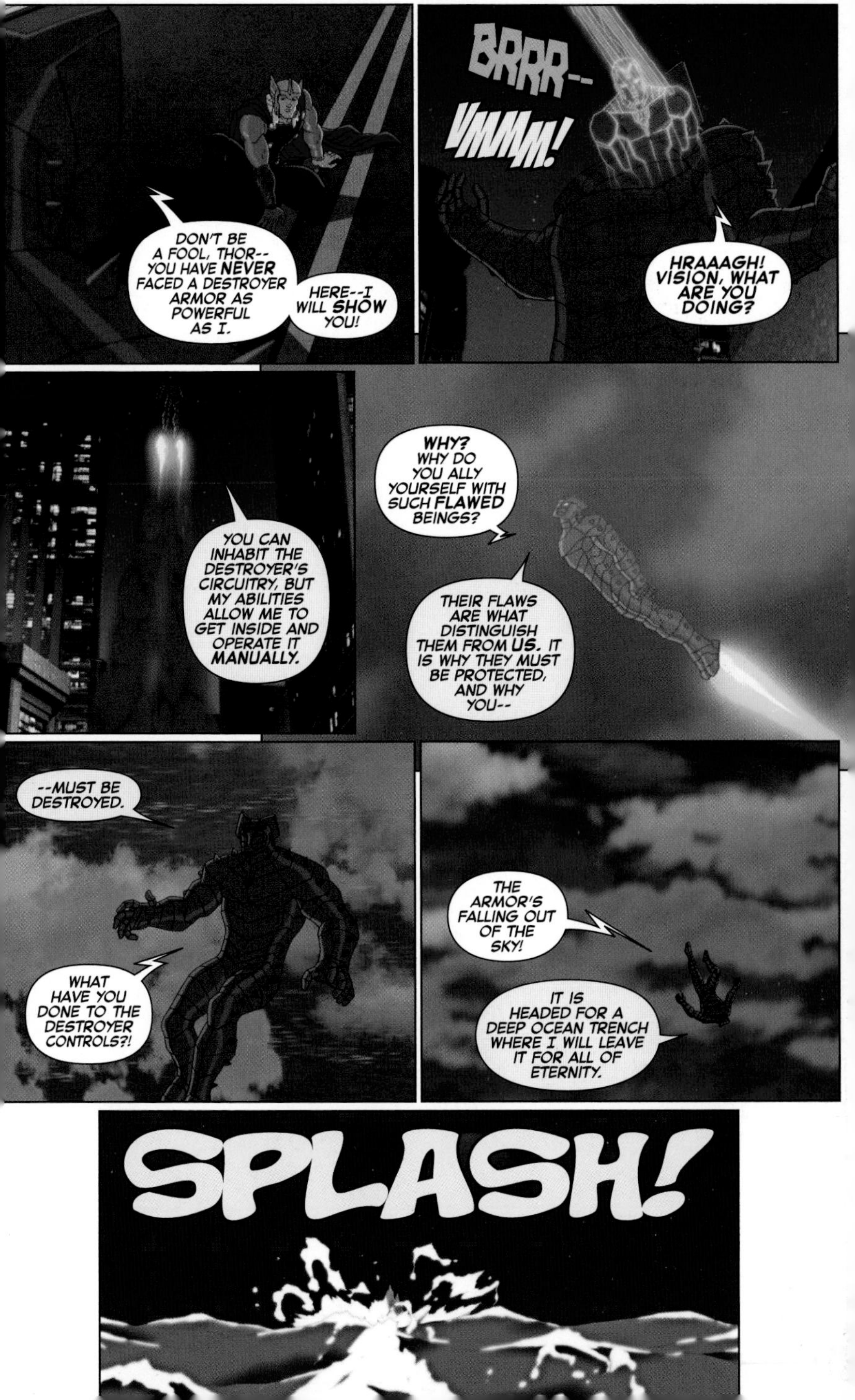
DON'T BE A FOOL, THOR-- YOU HAVE NEVER FACED A DESTROYER ARMOR AS POWERFUL AS I.
HERE--I WILL SHOW YOU!
BRRR--
VMMM!
HRAAAGH! VISION, WHAT ARE YOU DOING?
YOU CAN INHABIT THE DESTROYER'S CIRCUITRY, BUT MY ABILITIES ALLOW ME TO GET INSIDE AND OPERATE IT MANUALLY.
WHY? WHY DO YOU ALLY YOURSELF WITH SUCH FLAWED BEINGS?
THEIR FLAWS ARE WHAT DISTINGUISH THEM FROM US. IT IS WHY THEY MUST BE PROTECTED, AND WHY YOU--
--MUST BE DESTROYED.
WHAT HAVE YOU DONE TO THE DESTROYER CONTROLS?!
THE ARMOR'S FALLING OUT OF THE SKY!
IT IS HEADED FOR A DEEP OCEAN TRENCH WHERE I WILL LEAVE IT FOR ALL OF ETERNITY.
SPLASH!

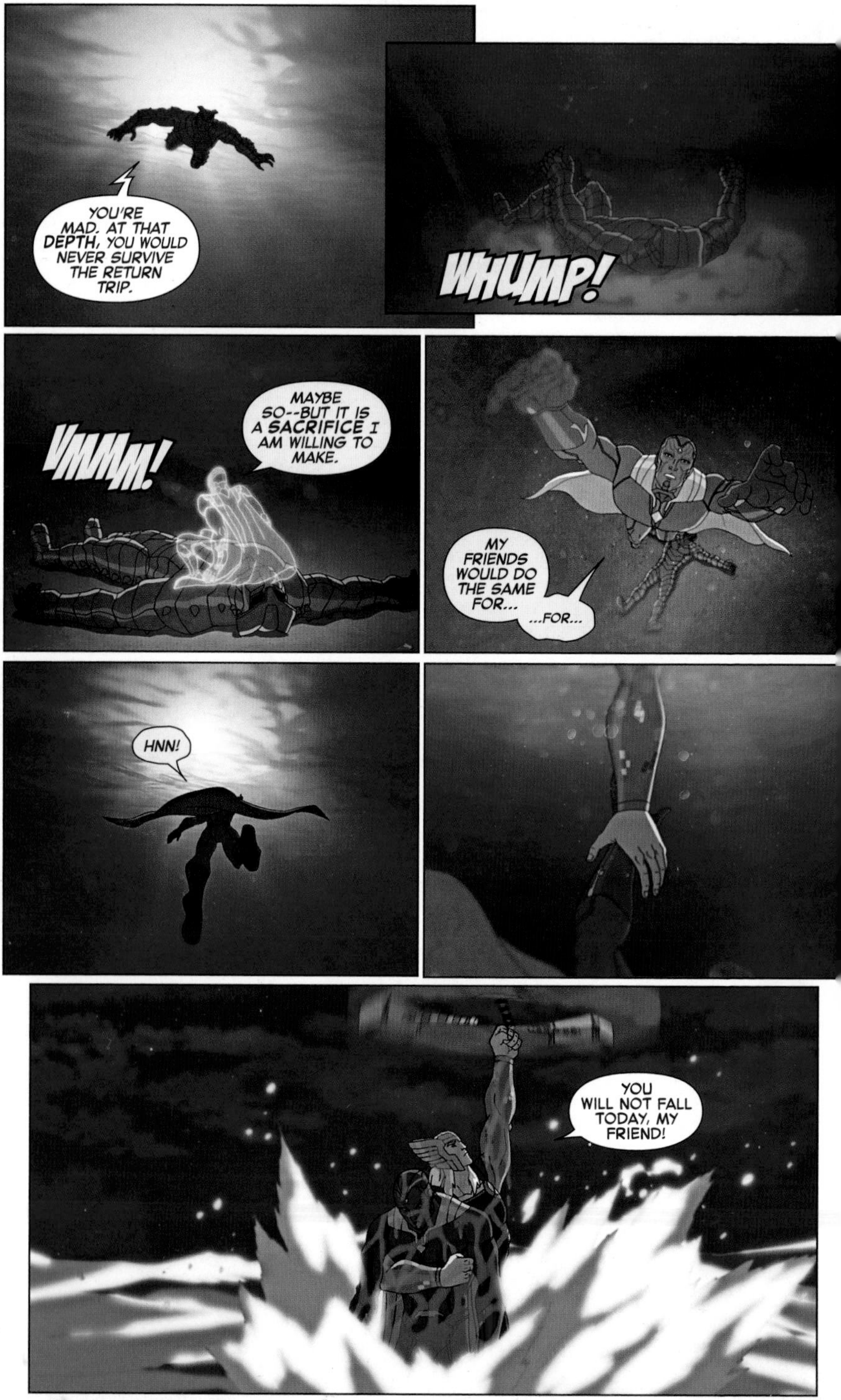
YOU'RE MAD. AT THAT DEPTH, YOU WOULD NEVER SURVIVE THE RETURN TRIP.
WHUMP!
VMMM!
MAYBE SO--BUT IT IS A SACRIFICE I AM WILLING TO MAKE.
MY FRIENDS WOULD DO THE SAME FOR...
...FOR...
HNN!
YOU WILL NOT FALL TODAY, MY FRIEND!

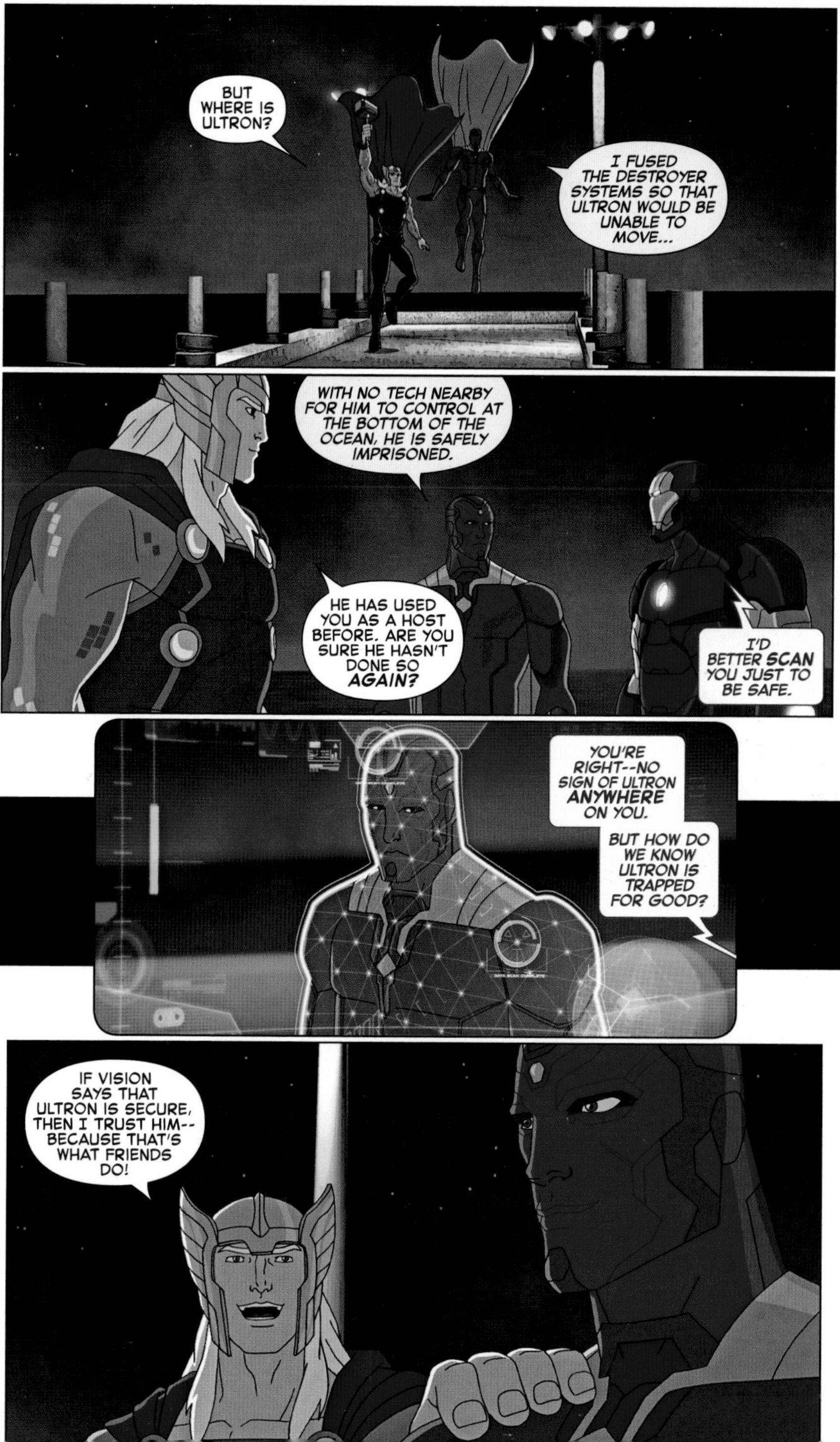
BUT WHERE IS ULTRON?
I FUSED THE DESTROYER SYSTEMS SO THAT ULTRON WOULD BE UNABLE TO MOVE...
WITH NO TECH NEARBY FOR HIM TO CONTROL AT THE BOTTOM OF THE OCEAN, HE IS SAFELY IMPRISONED.
HE HAS USED YOU AS A HOST BEFORE. ARE YOU SURE HE HASN'T DONE SO AGAIN?
I'D BETTER SCAN YOU JUST TO BE SAFE.
YOU'RE RIGHT--NO SIGN OF ULTRON ANYWHERE ON YOU.
BUT HOW DO WE KNOW ULTRON IS TRAPPED FOR GOOD?
IF VISION SAYS THAT ULTRON IS SECURE, THEN I TRUST HIM-- BECAUSE THAT'S WHAT FRIENDS DO!

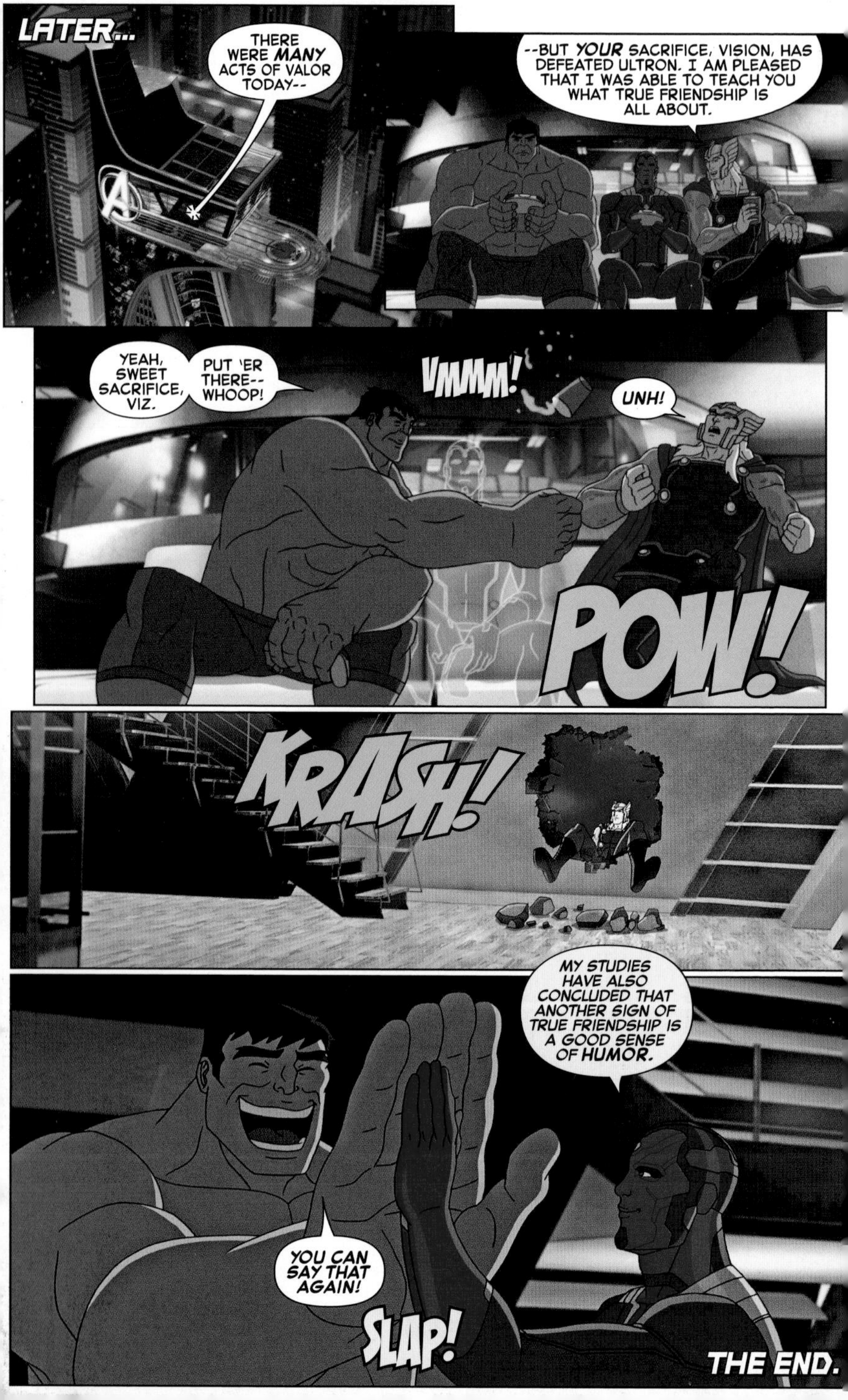
LATER...
THERE WERE MANY ACTS OF VALOR TODAY--
--BUT YOUR SACRIFICE, VISION, HAS DEFEATED ULTRON. I AM PLEASED THAT I WAS ABLE TO TEACH YOU WHAT TRUE FRIENDSHIP IS ALL ABOUT.
YEAH, SWEET SACRIFICE, VIZ.
PUT 'ER THERE--WHOOP!
VMMM!
UNH!
POW!
KRASH!
MY STUDIES HAVE ALSO CONCLUDED THAT ANOTHER SIGN OF TRUE FRIENDSHIP IS A GOOD SENSE OF HUMOR.
YOU CAN SAY THAT AGAIN!
SLAP!
THE END.

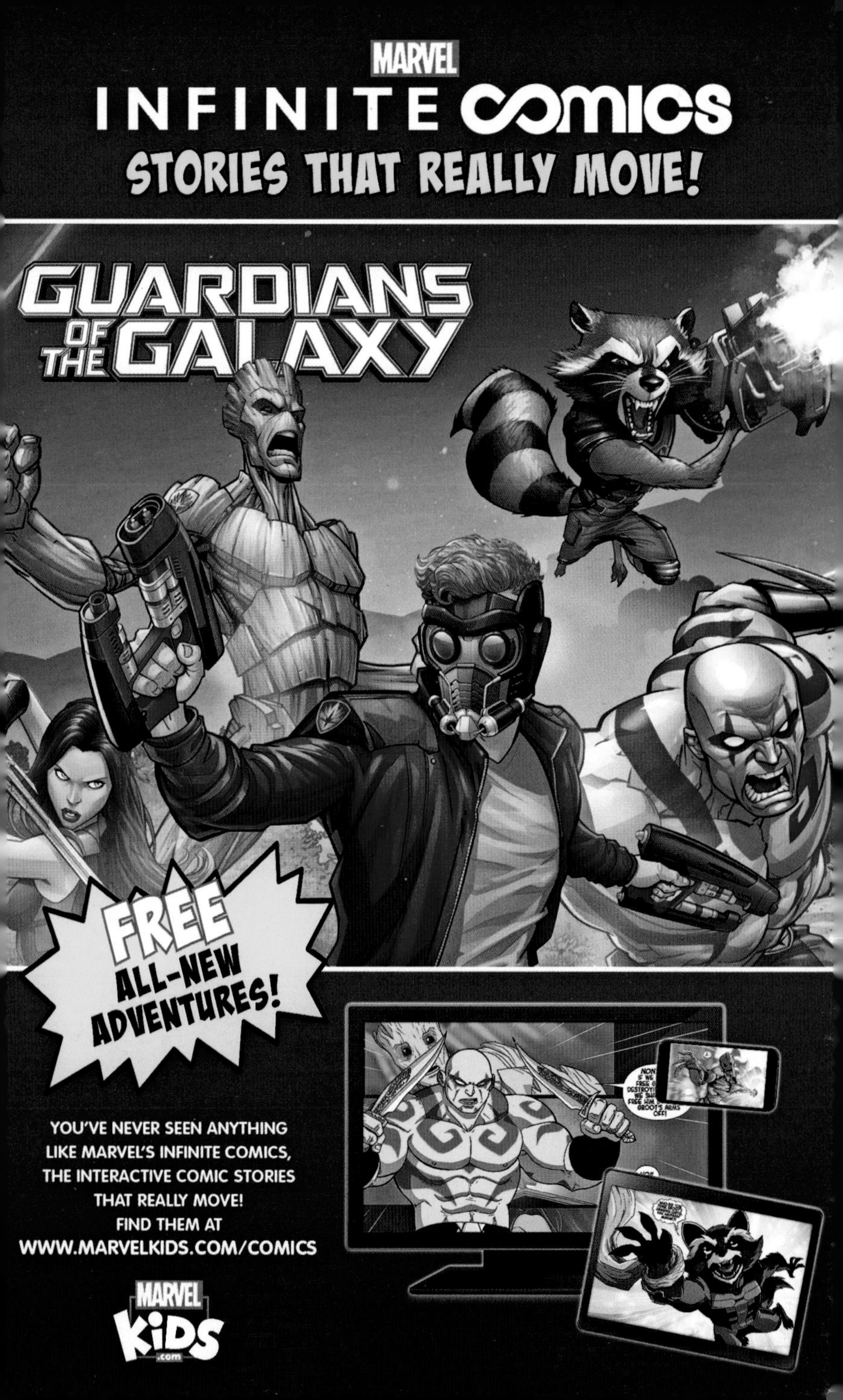
MARVEL
INFINITE COMICS
STORIES THAT REALLY MOVE!
GUARDIANS OF THE GALAXY
FREE ALL-NEW ADVENTURES!
YOU'VE NEVER SEEN ANYTHING LIKE MARVEL'S INFINITE COMICS, THE INTERACTIVE COMIC STORIES THAT REALLY MOVE! FIND THEM AT WWW.MARVELKIDS.COM/COMICS
MARVEL KiDS .com

WITNESS THE RISE OF ULTRON,
REIMAGINED AND RETOLD IN THRILLING
SOUTH KOREAN MANHWA STYLE!

MARVEL
AVENGERS K
AVENGERS VS. ULTRON

AVENGERS K BOOK 1: AVENGERS VS. ULTRON TPB

ISBN: 978-1-302-90120-2

COLLECTED IN ENGLISH FOR THE FIRST TIME!

AVAILABLE MAY 2016
IN PRINT AND DIGITAL WHEREVER BOOKS ARE SOLD

MARVEL

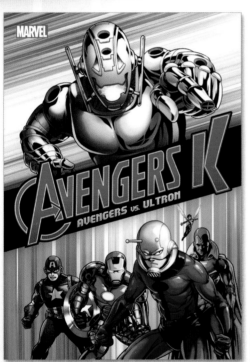

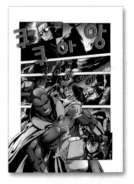

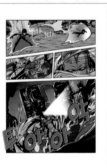

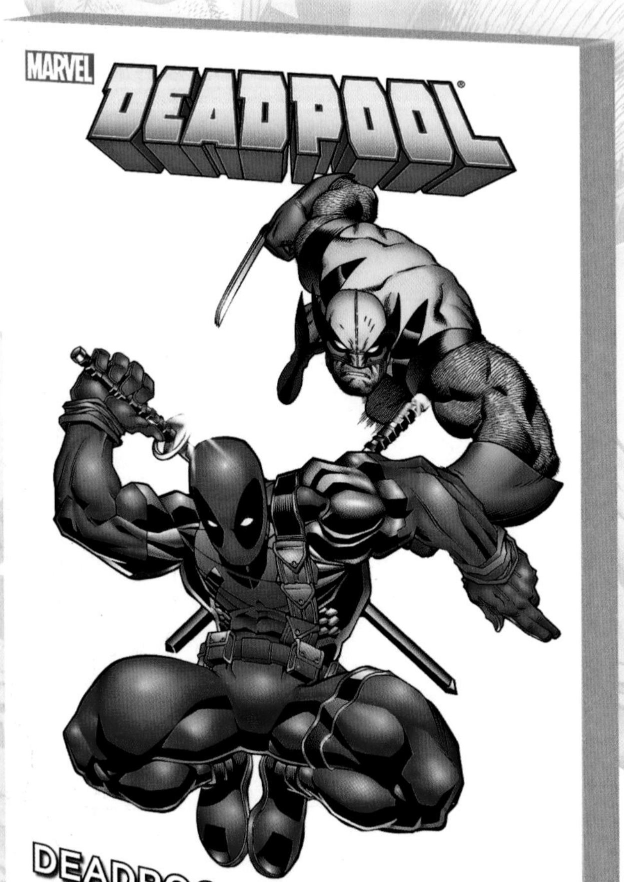
MARVEL
DEADPOOL
DEADPOOL & WOLVERINE